How to Make Passive Income through Crypto Mining

The Beginner's Guide on How to Make Money Online:

Bitcoin, NFT, Blockchain, Token in Real Estate, Yield Farm

Charlie Kent

Table of Contents:

INTRODUCTION

It's always good to bring in a little extra money on the side. Making money outside your day job can give your net worth a boost—it gives you some extra peace of mind.

In the twenty-something years of its existence, the internet has changed the world and people's lives in ways that no one could anticipate. Sending a message to someone on the other side of the planet is now a few clicks away as compared to sending letters, which would otherwise take days or even weeks before delivery. But there is more to the internet than emails and social media.

The internet itself is the biggest marketplace you can think of. With over 2 billion internet users worldwide, you can bet that this number of people would present a market for any serious entrepreneur willing to make a ton of profit through the internet. But since the ordinary Joe might not make another Google, Amazon or Facebook, it doesn't mean that all doors making money through the internet is concerned.

There are many other opportunities that you can exploit and make crazy money in the process. Forget about brick and mortar stores for a moment and think of how many opportunities exist when you can have your online store open 24/7 without increasing the number of personnel to take care of the night shifts. Forget about the overhead costs of running a brick-and-mortar store, and for one, think of the low operating cost of running an internet business.

You could run it from an island in Mauritius, from your home, from a coffee shop and from literally any part of the world. This increased flexibility and large market base present limitless growth and profit-making opportunities. You can also live the life you've always dreamed of because you will make money and have enough time to engage in many other activities.

With enough passive income, you no longer need to work and earn active income. You reach financial independence and can cover your living expenses solely with passive income streams from investments. At that point, you can spend your days travelling, playing golf, playing with your kids, volunteering, or working on passion projects.

LINEAR VS PASSIVE INCOME

You could be thinking about how to make money online and how to get wealthy through passive income. Is it feasible to become wealthy with passive income? Is this a legitimate method of earning money online? Or even if there is a way to make "simple passive money" online?

Many people may be sceptical that there is a way to accomplish this when so many scammers out there can separate you from your money. You can make money and even become wealthy online because it is the only form of generating money that is not dependent on you rearranging your schedule for a certain amount of money, or what is known as a paycheck. Unlike a paycheck, which is essentially exchanging your time for money, this type of internet income can help you become wealthy exactly because it is built on generating money frequently and in a passive manner that is received regularly. By definition, every passive income is unrelated to exchanging time for money.

The vast majority of people that work online do not make any money. They will never become wealthy through any means other than specific types of non-linear income, which can be earned with little or no out-of-pocket costs to the individual in many situations. Most affiliate networks offer affiliate blueprints for making money online that can eventually turn into passive income and allow someone to become wealthy—in many cases, developing an online business and generating steady, consistent income results from a thorough research, market identification, and appropriate and effective marketing techniques that generate sales and profits. Most good affiliate programs provide affiliates with the internet tools, ad text, and marketing opportunities they need to succeed. If they apply themselves to the goal of making money online, they will. Many people, however, observe the success of some affiliate marketers and believe that it is a simple way to earn a passive income when the reality is far from it.

Affiliates who wish to generate money through their affiliate programs while working from home can do so by following the blueprint given out for them by the program's operator. Individuals who previously worked for a paycheck or a line of credit and realized that it would not allow them to become wealthy chose to create an internet business that could be built to develop a passive income stream, if not several. Those who grasp the difference between passive and linear income are drawn to the Internet to make their goals come true.

Many people actively choose to work part-time before becoming full-time in the internet business and quitting their employment to build a second income that is a passive income rather than a second linear income. Get-rich-quick scams should be avoided at all costs, as they are not legitimate enterprises but rather a way to squander one's time on the Internet.

Let's explain what we mean by linear and passive income before looking at some of the most popular ways to make money online. This defines a linear income. As previously stated, linear income is obtained by either trading your time for money or working for someone else. To put it another way, the more you work, the more money you make. However, if you do not work, you will not earn money.

On the other hand, a passive income is a money that does not demand you to trade your time to create money. If you have taken steps to produce that income in the first place, a passive income will generate money for you whether you work or not. Once you've done that, your money will be paid to you regularly, not because you had to trade your time for it, but because you're being compensated for something you've already done, thus the term "passive income." Real estate profits, investing earnings, writing earnings, singing earnings [residuals], and making money from your web efforts are all examples of passive income. It can also come through online initiatives such as network marketing, affiliate marketing, and advertising. Cryptocurrency drew a lot of interest in 2018 to generate passive income. Making money with cryptocurrencies may be done in two ways. Trading and mining are two different things. The advantage of this technique is that it allows you to trade from your mobile device. Many people refer to this as "earning money while you sleep" and consider it easy passive income.

You will only be able to get wealthy if you have passive income. The more passive income you generate, the faster you will become wealthy. The source of all internet fortunes for those who get rich online is referred to as residuals by some. Some people believe that the key to internet success is to create as many separate streams of passive income as possible to diversify and safeguard one's interests. Once you've established one online passive income stream, it's much easier to set up another, then a third, and so on.

So, do you want to create a linear or a passive income?

The term "linear income" refers to the type of income that keeps you poor. It's akin to being an indentured servant if you trade your time for money. You work and are compensated for your efforts. You don't get paid if you don't work. It doesn't matter if you're a physician, a bank manager, a taxi driver, or a Walmart worker. These people have one thing in common: they exchange their time for a paycheck. They will not be paid if they cease working.

On the other hand, passive income is distinct in that it is revenue that you regularly receive for an action that you previously performed but no longer do. It's a source of income that you'll continue to receive even if you stop working. The more passive income streams you can create, the more money you'll generate and the faster you'll become wealthy.

The only way to get wealthy online is to promote affiliate programs that pay well and set up several of them to generate income. Remember, once you've built up your big money-making system, you won't have to micro-manage it to keep it working smoothly and generating more affiliate revenue. A set it and forget it system is truly the ultimate for successful online marketers who focus on properly setting up this system.

The choice is simple, and it is yours to make. Work once for a one-time payment, or work once for a lifetime payment. That is the slogan of affiliate marketers worldwide who understand the difference between linear and passive revenue streams and are always looking for new ways to develop income streams that will help them build their passive income over time.

The linear income stream is a struggle that many people believe they must endure earning a living. They go through the motions day after day, week after week, month after month, year after year, until their lives have passed them by, and they are grumbling about missed opportunities and how they have missed out on life.

On the other hand, passive income streams are not drudgery once set up and deliver an "easy income" of a passive type. They are regarded as divinely sent and are eagerly anticipated by the recipient. You can multitask while collecting passive money since you can be doing something else [like building up another passive income stream] while receiving this one.

Alternatively, you can spend time with your spouse, family, children, or friends doing things that interest you while knowing that your passive income stream is still paying you. You won't be able to do it with a linear income stream. You are not compensated if you prefer to spend time with your family rather than working. It's as simple as that.

Why anyone would choose to quit is perplexing, especially when you know that by repeating what you did to produce that revenue in the first place, you can repeat the process to generate another passive income stream. You can reclaim your life with a non-linear revenue stream [or two]. It provides comfort and security to know that you will receive it even if you cease doing what created it.

You should start generating your passive income stream as soon as possible if you are able. Start by doing it part-time and then gradually increase your workload. This is not a get-rich-quick strategy; thus, it will take time to mature. What does it matter if it takes you two, three, or even five years to get it right? However, if you do not begin to earn this form of revenue, you will be enslaved to a linear type of income that will only be available as long as you work. When you stop working, your income stops as well. A passive income, on the other hand, will continue to flow into your bank account even after you "retire."

Don't put it off. You will reap the benefits and gain control of your life the sooner you begin.

So, how can you increase your passive income?

Passive income can be divided into two categories. The first is investment income from a passive source. You must have cash available to invest in these income vehicles to obtain passive investment income. If you have money to invest, you should conduct adequate research and due diligence to determine which passive vehicles are the greatest fit for your situation and risk tolerance.

The second type of revenue comes from starting your own business with little or no money. For example, you may build a website that makes money from advertisements or join a network marketing company that will pay you even if you aren't actively operating the business. You might also establish your own business or work as an affiliate for someone else's.

You will most likely be able to produce income more rapidly if you have money to invest than if you don't. If you do not have any money to invest, you must be willing to provide time, energy, talents, resources, creativity, or all of these.

Focusing on the incremental increase, in my view, is the most practical strategy to earn passive income. Begin with a single modest step. Now is not the time to try to make an extra $10,000 per month in passive income. Concentrate on what you can do to produce $10 in passive revenue per month and go from there.

What are ten activities you could do in the next 30 days to produce $10 in passive income per month? What is one thing you can do this week to help yourself?

Why would you want to earn money that you don't have to work for?

You are financially free when your passive income exceeds their expenses. "Financially free" means that you do not need to work to cover your expenses during the day. After that, you're "free" to do whatever you want!

Is passive income considered investment income?

Earnings obtained from activities that do not involve active engagement are sometimes referred to as passive income.

Interest, dividends, and capital gains—investment earnings that don't need much active participation—are not classed as passive income by the Internal Revenue Service (IRS). They fall into the category of portfolio income instead.

Is it true that passive income is taxed?

Yes, the Internal Revenue Service (IRS) collects taxes on passive income. This type of income is frequently taxed at the same rate as wages from a job, though deductions can sometimes reduce the liability. It's a good idea to consult a tax professional for advice on how to minimize your tax obligations. They'll be able to advise you on how to take advantage of your unique circumstances.

CRYPTOCURRENCY LENDING

HOLDING isn't the only option to profit from Cryptocurrency without putting in any effort. Investors (as opposed to the always-stressed day traders) can earn interest on their bitcoin holdings in various methods, similar to earning interest on bank savings. However, many of these chances have been taken over by con artists. You might lose your Cryptocurrency just as quickly as you could make money with it.

Coin owners can lend their coins to the network to validate transactions. The network rewards you more the more coins you lend. Staking is a simple technique to earn passive income by receiving payment from the market for holding bitcoins for a set time. It provides a more predictable return on investment than other options, and unlike mining, it does not necessitate the purchase of hardware.

Despite the joys of passive income, there is no such thing as a free lunch when it comes to Crypto. While some are as simple as playing games to win Cryptocurrency, most of them require you to do your research and assess risk, prospective revenue, and other factors.

Crypto lending is a considerably newer method of profiting based on the concept of shorting. You don't need to comprehend the notion of shorting, but you should be aware that when you conduct this type of lending, you're lending your money to other traders who are also short traders. The beauty of crypto lending is that you won't have to worry about your money being stolen by the borrower. If the borrower does not pay their loans, the exchange will keep the funds and refuse to cash them out. There are many lending bots available, just like there are plenty of crypto trading bots, that allow investors to automate the loan process and put it on autopilot.

Cryptocurrency lending is the most straightforward way to earn money on your cryptocurrency holdings. Borrowers utilize your Cryptocurrency for trading, investment, or personal reasons, and you receive interest on a daily, weekly, monthly, or annual basis. Different types of crypto financing exist, each with its own set of risks and interest rates.

Crypto lending works similarly to peer-to-peer lending, where borrowers are connected with lenders via an online crypto lending platform with

Cryptocurrency as the currency of trade instead of fiat money. Lenders then provide the assets for these loans in exchange for interest rates on the asset. The main difference of each type of crypto lending is who or what is handling the lending and borrowing process, a business or a protocol. Centralized crypto lending platforms use margin lending to attract users; they offer favourable interest rates and terms to crypto lenders compared to decentralized crypto lending.

Crypto lending is a growing market that started only a few years ago. Unless you're new to Cryptocurrency, you probably have heard this term at some point. Crypto lending works similarly to peer-to-peer lending, where borrowers are connected with lenders via an online crypto lending platform with Cryptocurrency as the currency of trade instead of fiat money.

Individual investors or hodl-ers often use their crypto assets as collateral for cash loans used for investment or working capital. The mechanism may differ depending on the crypto lending platform. Still, to put it simply, borrowers use their crypto assets, such as bitcoin, as collateral to obtain a fiat loan or stable coin loan. Lenders then provide the assets for these loans in exchange for interest rates on the asset.

WHAT ARE THE DRAWBACKS OF CRYPTOCURRENCY LENDING?

If you decide to invest extensively in just one exchange, you'll be taking on more risk. The major downside is that you face the danger of losing all of your assets if the exchange goes out of business or takes your money. This has happened in the past, and it may happen again.

In both the controlled and decentralized portions of the crypto business, lending has become one of the most popular crypto services. You can lend your digital assets to borrowers for a chance to earn money as an investor. The main difference of each type of crypto lending is handling the lending and borrowing process; a business or a protocol. You have four major lending strategies to choose from.

PEER-TO-PEER LENDING:

Like P2P (peer-to-peer) trade systems connect buyers and sellers, the platform connects lenders with borrowers. Platforms that offer such services enable users to create their terms pick how much they want to lend and how much interest they want to earn on their loans. When it comes to crypto lending, such lending systems give customers a certain amount of power. You must, however, first put your digital asset into the loan platform's custodial wallet.

CRYPTOCURRENCY P2P LENDING

In recent years, the P2P lending market has continued to evolve with the introduction of Cryptocurrency, in particular, the Ethereum blockchain. Now, P2P lenders can utilize decentralized networks and smart contracts to open up new possibilities for accessing financial services outside of traditional banking infrastructure. This is what is commonly referred to as DeFi (decentralized finance).

Thanks to blockchain technology, borrowers and lenders may engage in a loan arrangement without the necessity for a middleman. With this tech, smart contracts are automatically executed as per the loan terms, enabling trustless transactions between both parties.

Like traditional P2P loans, loans that occur on the blockchain still require collateral, usually deposited in either fiat or digital currencies. In most cases, the collateral is held on an intermediary website or crypto P2P platform, where it will be held in a smart contract following the terms stipulated in the agreement.

The value of the collateral given decides the maximum quantity an individual can borrow. This is typically known as the collateral factor or collateral ratio. This system is implemented because there is no creditworthiness evaluation or history. After all, the lender generally does not reveal their identity. On the other side of the transaction, lenders earn interest from borrowers, usually set at a pre-agreed rate. In some cases, crypto P2P platforms offer incentives and other bonuses to lenders to attract more volume to their platform so that their lending ecosystem can function adequately.

These decentralized platforms make lending available to anyone with access to the internet and sufficient funds to put down as collateral. These services are open 24 hours a day, seven days per week, and operate much more efficiently than traditional banking services. It is one of the reasons for the massive surge in popularity over the past couple of years.

Furthermore, there is no need for any KYC process, which means that lenders and borrowers can interact anonymously, which would have been thought impossible in the not-so-distant past.

One of the main criticisms of Crypto P2P lending is the steep learning curve associated with the process, especially for those unfamiliar with the fundamentals of cryptocurrency transactions. The UX of most major platforms is relatively clunky, and there is still an element of uncertainty towards the safety and security of these platforms. Unfortunately, many of the major lending platforms have experienced hacks and exploits in some respect, which has caused both lenders and borrowers to lose funds and suffer financial losses.

CENTRALIZED LENDING:

In this technique, you rely entirely on third-party lending infrastructure. Interest rates and lock-up periods are both fixed in this case. To begin earning interest, you must transfer your Crypto to the lending platform, just as you would with P2P lending.

They are entities or companies that handle the user's onboarding process, such as implementing KYC (Know-Your-Customer) and exchanging cryptocurrencies and fiat money with a custodial system to protect the assets. They are also more flexible in forming partnerships with other businesses and negotiating customized loan agreements.

Centralized crypto lending platforms use margin lending to attract users. They offer to maximize the productivity of their crypto assets safely and easily. Furthermore, it is also common for them to offer favourable interest rates and terms to crypto lenders compared to decentralized crypto lending.

DECENTRALIZED LENDING

Decentralized lending, often known as DeFi lending, is a mechanism that allows users to conduct lending transactions directly on the blockchain. DeFi lending does not require any intermediaries, unlike P2P and centralized lending schemes. Instead, lenders and borrowers deal through smart contracts, programmable and self-executing contracts that adjust interest rates autonomously and regularly.

Decentralized crypto lending, often known as DeFi, is managed by a series of protocols (decentralized finance). Smart contracts are used in the protocols to automate the distribution of crypto loans and interest payments. The loan and borrowing operations in centralized crypto lending are entrusted to a firm or a group of persons.

DeFi platforms are often non-custodial, do not require KYC, and focus solely on cryptocurrencies. The interest rates offered to vary depending on market supply and demand; nonetheless, they are typically lower than those offered by centralized platforms. Because anybody can access the protocols and the transactions are recorded on public blockchains, DeFi is more transparent than centralized.

Even though crypto markets are still relatively new and have only been operating for a few years, crypto financing has a lot of potentials. It is a new concept that has piqued the interest of cryptocurrency investors and dealers. Whether you choose to participate in centralized or decentralized lending, you can expect to see more projects in both areas as bitcoin deposits and loan productivity continue to rise.

.MARGIN LENDING

Last but not least, you might lend your crypto assets to traders who want to trade with borrowed funds. These traders use borrowed cash to increase their trading position and then repay the loans with interest. In this instance, crypto exchanges handle most of the job for you. You only need to make your digital item accessible.

WHAT IS CRYPTO MARGIN LENDING, AND HOW DOES IT WORK?

Margin trading is an option for crypto traders with limited resources, such as Altcoins and Bitcoins, to increase leverage on their investment. This can help raise the amount invested without holding the assets. It's worth mentioning that margin trading isn't for everyone, and it comes with a high level of risk.

WHAT IS MARGIN TRADING, AND HOW DOES IT WORK?

Margin trading allows a trader to open a position backed by leverage. For instance, we've placed a 2x leveraged margin position. Then we increased our basic assets to 10%. As a result of the 2x leverage, our position yielded 20 percent. The most common trades are done with a 1:1 leverage.

Margin trading is very viable thanks to the existence of a loan market. Many lenders are eager to lend money to traders to invest more in coins and exchanges, while lenders profit from the interest on the loans. Users offer loans for margin markets on other exchanges, such as Poloniex, while the exchange itself provides them on others. For example, with the Poloniex exchange, anyone can lend their altcoins or Bitcoins and profit from the interest earned on loan. The most significant downside is that the coins must be kept in the exchange's wallet, which is less safe than a cold wallet.

MARGIN TRADING'S COSTS AND RISKS

As previously indicated, the cost of a margin position includes paying the interest on borrowed coins, whether to the exchange or other users. It also necessitates fees to open a position on the exchange. Remember that as the potential to gain more money grows, so does the potential to lose more. The most you can lose is the entire amount you put into starting a position for the exchange. This level is known as the liquidation value, and it is the point at which the exchange will cancel your position instantly, allowing you to lose only your own money rather than the entire loaded amount.

When we talk about regular trading and leverage of 1:1, for example, the value of liquidation is only when the position reaches zero. The liquidation value will get closer to the buying price as leverage rises. For example, the value of Bitcoin is $1,000, and we have purchased one Bitcoin with a 2:1 leverage. Our position will cost us $1,000 in total, plus we will borrow another $1,000. The position's liquidation value will be a little more than USD 500 because we have already lost our USD 1,000, plus interest and fees, at that level. Margin trading can also be used to trade against the market, and we may take a short position using leverage.

When it comes to margin trading, there are a few aspects that customers should consider:

Maintaining a sense of fairness

The trading platform will always demand traders to maintain a certain level of equity, which is usually set at 30%. If your balance falls below this level, you will be asked to deposit additional funds into your account to restore your equity. If you are unable or unwilling to deposit funds, the brokerage will be compelled to terminate your position to improve the account's equity.

Profits may be outstripped by interest.

Margin trading can be profitable, especially when employed for short-term investments. If you invest money and don't see the expected increase in value, consider cutting your losses and paying the short-term interest rates. Allowing your margin trading position to remain open for an extended period may result in losses, even if the value of your equities rises. The reason for this is that margin trading has high-interest rates, and your profits may not be enough to cover the loan you took out.

You could lose a lot more than you already have.

Margin trading does more than just increase profits. It also exaggerates losses. If something goes wrong, you'll not only lose your money, but you'll also be in trouble since you'll have to pay back the money you borrowed from the broker plus interest. If you're not careful, you may end up with a lot of debt. You should also remember that margin accounts are frequently more sensitive than ordinary trading accounts due to daily market fluctuations.

Margin trading gains an element of unpredictability as a result of this.

TRADING STRATEGIES FOR MARGIN

Management of Risk

When it comes to margin trading, it's critical to establish clear risk management guidelines and be mindful of excessive greed. Consider how much you're willing to risk, and keep in mind that you could lose everything. **Keep an eye on things.**

Cryptocurrency margin trading carries a twofold risk. Cryptocurrencies are a sort of asset that is extremely volatile. As a result, consider using leveraged bets for short-term trading. Furthermore, while the margin position and daily fees are currently insignificant, they may eventually become important in the long run.

Movements of Extremes

Extreme volatility in both directions might occur in crypto trading at times. The danger is that the deep might reach our liquidation value when it comes to this. This is more common when the leverage is high, and the liquidation value is close. You can profit from these deeps by setting a closing target position and hoping that the deep will go over them, leaving you with a decent profit and eventually returning to the original price.

IS MARGIN TRADING RIGHT FOR YOU?

Except if you've done a lot of studies or have a lot of experience, we strongly advise you to avoid margin trading. It's aggravating enough to lose money when trading bitcoin without borrowing money to construct leveraged positions. This has the potential to exacerbate the stress level.

If you're less traditional than us and still want to margin trade, the next step is to study all margin trading documentation for a given exchange. You should understand about opening and closing margin positions, as well as calls and margin ratios, and at the very least try to brush up on some margin trading strategy specifics.

MARGIN-TRADING-ENABLED EXCHANGES

Crypto traders should keep the number of coins on the exchange minimum. Most exchanges now allow you to trade margin. The primary advantage of leveraged trading is obvious, but security is also a significant consideration. This is because hackers frequently target exchanges, and there have been multiple hacking incidents on exchanges recently.

Margin trading allows us to raise our stake without providing the necessary Bitcoin. For example, suppose our portfolio contains five Bitcoins, and we want to protect ourselves against the risk of Bitcoins falling in value. In that case, we can open a 10X leveraged short position equivalent to 40% of our portfolio. The amount needed to open the position will be a tenth of it or ten times the leverage. This implies we'll need roughly 0.2 Bitcoins on hand, and they'll be held safely in cold wallets. We'd be able to keep fewer coins in the exchange account this way.

Bitmex is a cryptocurrency exchange.

Bitmex has had a strong reputation for a long time, and many traders use it regularly. This exchange, which is at the forefront of margin trading, offers up to 100X leverage in short- and long-term margin trading. It's also incredibly easy to use, and they provide excellent customer service. Upon registration, you may be eligible for a 10% discount on trading fees for the first six months.

Plus500

Plus500 is a fully regulated international firm. You can trade CFDs on Forex stocks, options, indexes, and commodities if you have a Plus500 account.

They have Bitcoins and Altcoins for large trading in crypto margin trading. The fact that they are a completely regulated firm is their major advantage. Furthermore, they provide excellent customer service and are responsible to millions of clients. You can also enrol and start margin trading right away with a bank transfer or a credit card deposit. Margin leverage of 1:2 can be put up, and it usually goes well at first because a sample account can be set up for free.

Bitfinex

This exchange works with the largest trading volume in the Bitcoin US dollar market and margin trading with 3.3X leverage.

It has a user-friendly layout, and simple transactions are straightforward to complete.

Poloniex is one of the most popular cryptocurrency exchanges.

They do not have any BTC US dollar margin trading while having leveraged trading of 11 altcoins. Only 2.5X leverage is offered, and they frequently charge a large interest cost when shorting.

AvaTrade

Another well-known CFD exchange allows you to trade Bitcoin CFDs and other major cryptocurrencies. It's regulated and offers a free sample account, just like Plus500.

Ratios Should Be Used With Caution

Trading cryptocurrency on margin is one of the riskiest wagers you'll ever make. Cryptocurrency is dangerous in and of itself, but margin trading has increased the risk. You could easily find yourself owing a large sum of money. Margin trading, unlike conventional trading, has the potential to cause you to lose your whole initial investment. Furthermore, the more leverage you have, the more likely you will lose it. For example, if you go long on a 4:1 margin and then the position drops to roughly 25% or even less because you'll almost certainly have to pay some fees, the margin will be called in, and you'll be left with nothing.

Margin trading is only profitable if the investment you make allows you to pay off your loans plus any interest you may have accrued. If you're contemplating betting on margin, you might want to start small and learn from your mistakes. Margin trading isn't all bad. It may be a helpful investment tool if the risks are minimal.

IS IT POSSIBLE TO BORROW OR LEND CRYPTOCURRENCY?

When you think of Crypto, the first thing that springs to mind is 'holding.' Many people mistakenly believe that cryptocurrency ownership is akin to stock ownership. According to such beliefs, you should buy and retain your Crypto until the asset's price rises significantly. However, for earning interest on their crypto assets, many people turn to the most popular crypto lending platform they can find.

With the significantly increased levels of attention towards the DeFi movement, crypto financing has been more prevalent in recent times. Without deviating from our topic, let us first answer the question, "What are crypto lending platforms?" before moving on to the best alternatives.

Lending in Cryptocurrency

It's critical to understand crypto lending before moving on in your search for the safest crypto lending platform. Crypto lending is essentially a means of lending crypto assets or fiat currency to borrowers at a fixed interest rate. As a result, crypto lending resembles the loan procedure in regular banking systems.

The two most prominent aspects of the crypto loan procedure demonstrate the parallels with traditional banking. You have lenders with many cryptocurrencies and seek ways to make money passively. On the other hand, borrowers typically require loans secured by crypto assets they own.

On the other hand, the cryptocurrency lending platform clearly distinguishes crypto lending from regular lending. The lending platform is a critical component in crypto lending because it is the major facilitator of loans.

CRYPTO LENDING PLATFORMS: WHAT ARE THEY, AND HOW DO THEY WORK?

You should now be able to distinguish different sorts of crypto lending platforms now that you know the answer to the question "What are crypto lending platforms?" CeFi and DeFi platforms, for example, are two distinct sorts of platforms for lending cryptos.

Platforms CeFi

In most cases, CeFi or centralized finance platforms act as intermediaries in the crypto loan process. A centralized cryptocurrency lending platform would take ownership of lenders' assets and borrowers' collateral for the loan duration. Furthermore, a centralized crypto lending site would necessitate a KYC process, removing anonymity.

Platforms for DeFi

On the other hand, DeFi, or decentralized finance platforms, offer a decentralized approach to crypto lending. DeFi platforms use smart contracts to carry out lending procedures. Most importantly, DeFi lending platforms might provide complete automation of the lending process and contract execution if certain conditions are met.

THE ACCOUNT THAT PAYS INTEREST

Some platforms allow you to earn interest on stored crypto assets the same as on fiat currency in a traditional interest-bearing account.

Hodlnaut is one of the most popular of these services. It pays daily interest rates of up to 12.73 percent, earned by lending your funds on margin to crypto traders. Hodlnaut, based in Singapore, is still obtaining a license and being fully regulated.

When crypto holders deposit assets in a special interest-earning account at some popular crypto exchanges, they can receive an annual rate. Interest rates of around 6% p.a. are common, and Crypto is lent on interest to both individual and institutional borrowers.

HOW DOES CRYPTO LENDING WORK?

When you're looking for a crypto loan platform, the largest one can attract your eye right away. However, you should understand how crypto loan platforms work to choose the best choice for your needs. Focusing on the role of various components is the best way to learn how a top crypto lending platform works.

Lenders play an important role in the crypto lending process as donors. They deposit their crypto assets for a set or variable term to earn passive income on them.

Borrowers must use their crypto assets as security and take out loans against them rather than selling them. Borrowers must also pay interest on borrowed loans to recoup their collateral.

The bitcoin lending platform acts as a regulatory framework for the lending and borrowing process. As you may have noted, the platform can be centralized or decentralized. Matching orders, liquidity pools, or codes may be used to regulate the lending process, depending on the type of platform.

LIST OF CRYPTO LENDING SITES

Are you looking for the finest cryptocurrency loan platforms? Let's get started! Here is a list of the finest crypto loan platforms with a brief explanation.

Cryptocurrency is the most popular keyword in the financial and technological worlds. Crypto has introduced fresh perspectives on financial services based on the power of blockchain technology. Surprisingly, Crypto has recently achieved widespread appeal, resulting in the rapid development of a slew of new methods for extracting value from crypto assets.

Crypto lending is one of the most famous strategies for getting additional value from your crypto holdings in recent times. It is critical to comprehend the worth of crypto lending efficiently as the quest for the finest crypto lending platform becomes a top priority for crypto investors. Apart from a thorough understanding of the principles of crypto lending, it's critical to recognize the critical aspects that may help you choose the best crypto lending platform quickly.

The following discussion provides a detailed outline of a crypto lending platforms list and a brief overview of each platform. You can also thoroughly understand the key criteria to consider when choosing a cryptocurrency loan platform.

HOW SHOULD CRYPTO LENDING PLATFORMS BE PICKED?

Before going over a crypto lending platforms list, the last thing you should do is make a list of crucial elements to consider while making your decision. Here are some of the most important aspects to consider when choosing a crypto lending platform.

Rates of Interest

The interest rate offered by a crypto loan platform is the most important thing to consider when choosing one. The expenses associated with different crypto assets on different platforms are major in determining the best crypto loan platform. Choose a lending platform that will pay you a reasonable interest rate on your crypto assets.

Platform Threats

Before deciding on a crypto loan platform, you should consider the platform's dangers.

Term of the Loan

When looking for the safest crypto lending platform, it's also vital to consider the loan period. Check to see if the loan term is fixed or variable, and then decide based on your needs.

Amount of Collateral

Another significant consideration when selecting a crypto loan platform is the collateral required to borrow a specific amount.

Deposit Requirements

The deposit limit is the final consideration when selecting the best crypto loan platform for your needs. Check with the platform to see if there are any special restrictions for a minimum deposit amount.

PLATFORMS FOR CRYPTO LENDING

You might be eager to identify the most popular crypto lending platform after reading a full analysis of the foundations of crypto lending platforms. Here are some of the most popular crypto lending platforms available today.

Celsius

When it comes to the most popular crypto loan platform, Celsius is undoubtedly the first name that comes to mind. It allows you to make almost a 17 percent return on your Cryptocurrency by lending it. It's worth noting that there are no fees associated with borrowing, moving, or lending coins on Celsius.

Additionally, holders of the CEL token, Celsius's native token, may receive a 25% bonus. Furthermore, Celsius allows you to use your Cryptocurrency as collateral and borrow money at low rates.

Compound

Compound, the most prominent crypto lending platform on the market right now, serves as a model for several newer businesses. Many cryptocurrencies are listed on the protocol, and users can borrow or deposit the ones they want. The Compound also has its native token, COMP, enabling you to earn better returns by lending your Cryptocurrency to the platform to improve liquidity.

Compound's most intriguing feature is that it is currently the safest crypto lending platform available. Furthermore, Compound's live price feed enables easy and flexible tracking of prices on platforms based on available liquidity.

Binance

Binance is certainly one of the top entries in a crypto lending platforms list, given that it is the world's largest crypto exchange. Binance has created its ecosystem and its well-known function as a prominent cryptocurrency exchange.

Binance may now be used to receive a loan on your crypto assets or to lend your crypto assets. The network has launched its native coin, "BNB," to promote DeFi adoption worldwide. To put it another way, Binance is a onestop-shop for buying, selling, exchanging, and even trading crypto assets.

Alchemix is a cryptocurrency loan platform.

In the DeFi area, Alchemix is another excellent example of a top crypto lending platform. It takes a one-of-a-kind approach to crypto financing, making loans that can be repaid over time. Users must put DAI into a smart contract to obtain a token.

Smart contracts deposit deposited assets in a Yearn vault, in charge of DAI minting. The token, also known as aIUSD, represents the DAI deposit's future yield farming potential. The aIUSD debt of Alchemix customers lowers when the yield is harvested. As a result, the borrowers' collateral on Alchemix might be used to repay the loan.

CoinLoan is a service that allows you to borrow money in the form of coins

CoinLoan is yet another promising example of the greatest cryptocurrency loan platform. It's a trustworthy crypto lending platform that works well with iOS and Android while managing digital assets. On CoinLoan, you won't have to worry about fees for deposits or withdrawals.

CoinLoan, for example, gives you the chance to earn daily interest on your crypto assets. The biometric authentication employed in CoinLoan apps ensures that any crypto assets in your control are more secure.

Platforms for bitcoin financing created by Blockfi

In terms of features, the largest crypto loan platform is always intriguing. Blockfi, on the other hand, has some unique features for a crypto lending platform, such as an 8.5 percent annual percentage yield on various crypto assets. Most importantly, there are no minimum balance requirements or hidden fees on the platform.

Blockfi is, without a doubt, the best crypto lending platform for people with varying levels of experience in the field. You can earn more simply by storing your crypto assets in a single location. Within a few simple steps, crypto holders can borrow funds from the site at a rate of 4.5 percent APR.

AAVE

A list of crypto lending platforms would be incomplete without mentioning AAVE, the popular decentralized liquidity protocol. AAVE is a non-custodial system that allows all users to earn interest on their crypto holdings while borrowing funds by staking their crypto assets. AAVE offers a variety of services in addition to lending and borrowing. Users may get a clear picture of interest rates and access to additional features like flash loans and bug bounty.

Platforms for crypto financing YouHodler

YouHodler is one of the first to debate the most popular crypto lending site. It can let users get crypto loans in any of the top 15 cryptocurrencies with a loan-to-value ratio of around 90%. In exchange for staking Crypto as collateral, the site gives quick payments. YouHodler also converts assets into various forms and pay users interest for depositing their Crypto on the platform.

MakerDAO

With its native token, DAI, MakerDAO is also one of the top entries as the largest crypto lending platform, with no limits on its use. On MakerDAO, users could deposit over 25 crypto assets as collateral in the vault. You can borrow DAI against your platform contribution or get additional collateral to increase your risk. Simply connect your cryptocurrency wallet to MakerDAO, and you've got yourself a powerful crypto lending platform.

MoneyToken

MoneyToken would undoubtedly be the final entry as the best crypto lending platform. It can assist users in easily managing their crypto assets and receiving crypto-backed loans. Users can choose loan terms while also benefiting from the benefits of decentralization. As a result, you can have complete ownership and control over the assets at stake.

People venturing into the crypto world would try to find out "What are crypto lending platforms?" for obvious reasons. However, it is important to understand that crypto lending is different from traditional lending, albeit with distinct functionalities. For example, crypto lending platforms offer the possibilities for complete independence from banks and centralized institutions in the lending process.

Even if crypto lending platforms are popular and offer lucrative interest rates, it is important to evaluate every alternative carefully. Apart from reviewing every crypto lending platform in this list, you should also take note of the important factors required for crypto lending platforms.

CLOUD MINING

Unlike the proof-of-stake mechanism described previously, some blockchains use a more computer-intensive approach, such as Bitcoin. Cloud mining, like third-party proof-of-staking, allows you to mine Cryptocurrency without owning or maintaining a crypto mining gear. While contentious and hazardous, Cloud mining allows crypto holders to rent mining hardware from dedicated mining farms and receive mining fees. The mining companies charge a daily maintenance fee in exchange.

Although it may appear to be a good deal, cloud mining is a very risky proposition. Mining has very low-profit margins, and some cloud mining companies take up to a year to pay out earned profits. The crypto asset being mined could decline in value throughout that time, making it unprofitable to mine. The mining company cancels the contract in such circumstances.

Scams abound in cloud mining, resulting in significant losses for those wanting to earn a quick buck. Due to the venture's distant location and nearcomplete lack of regulation, extensive due diligence is required before investing.

Genesis Mining and HashNest are two well-known cloud mining companies.

Cryptocurrency mining verifies and adds transactions between users to the blockchain public ledger. Mining is also responsible for adding new coins to the existing circulating supply. One of the main components allows cryptocurrencies to function as a decentralized peer-to-peer network without a central authority. Proof of Work is a consensus algorithm used in mining (PoW).

The most well-known method of generating a passive income using bitcoin is mining. Although Bitcoin is the most well-known and well-established example of a mineable cryptocurrency, none are mineable.

Crypto mining is the term for this technique. Users must prove their claim's eligibility to become validators (also known as miners) by competing against each other to solve highly complex mathematical puzzles. Miners must invest in powerful computers and pay excessive electricity rates due to the competitiveness of this consensus mechanism.

This project is unquestionably time-consuming and complicated. As a result, investors frequently choose cloud mining as an alternative. You can use this to pay third companies to handle the technical aspects of crypto mining for you. In essence, you pay a one-time fee to a platform that provides such services to rent or buy mining devices from their mining facility. Following this initial payment, you may be required to pay a daily maintenance charge to the cloud mining service provider for them to assist you in managing your mining rigs.

Since its widespread use, cloud mining has been a source of contention. As exhilarating as this may sound, it is fraught with danger. Due to the remote location of this mining enterprise, there have been multiple examples of scams. As a result, you should do your homework before choosing this option. The first thing to understand is that crypto-currencies are real, and mining them is a perfectly legal and worldwide practised enterprise. It relies on computers to solve difficult mathematical problems to release the next chain of coins into circulation.

Mining bitcoins and MLM (Multi-Level Marketing) enterprises are entirely legal worldwide. Cloud miners guarantee to pay you interest if you invest in their mining operations or purchase a particular amount of hash power at a mining facility (e.g., Bitclub Network). These two notions are largely combined in the latest bitcoin mining revenue potential wave. When you combine the two, you have a legitimate legal passive income opportunity based on a real product with a real compensation plan for the first time on the internet.

CLOUD MINING: HOW TO MAKE A CONSISTENT PASSIVE INCOME

Cloud mining is a far more secure way to invest in cryptocurrencies and receive consistent passive income as an investment alternative. But how are you going to accomplish it?

The rise of Bitcoin – both as traditional currencies and as platforms for other, far more complex financial products – has been spectacular, and it has brought with it investment opportunities. However, because of the volatile nature of cryptocurrencies, investing and profiting in them is vulnerable to crypto volatility.

There is a technique to create consistent, passive income with cryptocurrency investment that isn't all "high risk, high reward." Isn't it intriguing?

Cloud mining is a far more secure way to invest in cryptocurrencies and receive consistent passive income as an investment alternative.

WHAT IS CLOUD MINING, AND HOW DOES IT WORK?

Mining creates more of the finite quantity of Bitcoins or other altcoins like Ethereum and Litecoin through a computational process. When miners successfully demonstrate proof of performing complex computations in Blockchain algorithms ahead of others, they are rewarded with these coins.

However, as the value of cryptos grew, manufacturing them grew more complicated. Unfortunately, the energy and computational power requirements of running a sustainable mining operation were soon to put it beyond individual effort, especially for those using it as one of their several income streams.

WHY IS CLOUD MINING THE BEST WAY TO EARN PASSIVE INCOME?

As a result, the following are the most important reasons:

The headaches of buying and operating expensive equipment to manage a data centre for a mining business should not be part of earning passive money. All you have to do with cloud mining is take use of cloud mining sites' services, and you'll be well on your way to earning a good return on your investment.

Crypto enthusiasts and non-techies are welcome to attend: You won't have to deal with technical equipment or environments if you use cloud mining. Furthermore, even non-tech knowledgeable individuals interested in the money-making aspect of Blockchain algorithms can earn here by simply subscribing to proxy mining services offered by various Bitcoin cloud mining sites.

Flexible investment possibilities: When it comes to cloud mining, you have a lot of alternatives when it comes to which Cryptocurrency you should invest in. You can invest in any of

Bitcoin, Ethereum, or Litecoin, or you can spread your money across all three to avoid placing all your eggs in one basket.

Binding contracts provide a greater sense of security: Cloud mining contracts provide security to both crypto-savvy and non-tech savvy investors by allowing them to know what to expect from each investment regarding hashing power rates and longevity.

IS IT POSSIBLE TO MAKE MONEY WITH CLOUD MINING?

You've probably heard about crypto mining, whether you own 35 bitcoins or are just getting started. It's a lengthy procedure to remove the word "financial" from the investment equation.

You've probably heard about crypto mining, whether you own 35 bitcoins or are just getting started. It's a lengthy procedure to remove the word "financial" from the investment equation.

Unfortunately, people frequently waste more time and money than they earn. One reason for this is that mining isn't as simple as everyone makes it out to be. It takes a lot of effort, in addition to having super-powerful hardware and a lot of time and energy.

Mining used to be possible for anyone interested back when bitcoin wasn't so pricey. You might call yourself a miner with just a pair of respectable graphics cards and a month's worth of power.

Things became a little more complicated as enthusiasts became professionals and professionals became organizations. Mining became a communal activity since it was so tough and time-consuming. People would band together to pay the bill for computing power and split the profits. They dubbed it pool mining, and it eventually became the only way to generate Cryptocurrency.

Even pool mining isn't efficient enough these days. Some of us don't have time to think about hardware, ASICs, electricity expenses, or anything else. Those people, and their need for convenience, inspired cloud mining.

Unlike traditional mining, which tries to avoid the financial aspect of crypto investments, cloud mining places it front and centre. You are now investing money rather than time and effort. A cloud mining user would pay for a share of the operational capacity, or hash power (H), and receive Cryptocurrency in proportion to their investment.

Does it appear to be overly simple? That's all there is to it. The goal is to make it as simple as possible to earn Cryptocurrency passively. However, how much they make is a different topic.

HOW MUCH CAN A CLOUD MINING COMPANY PAY YOU?

According to blockchaininfo.org's current data, roughly 1,800 Bitcoins are mined daily. We could get a daily cloud bitcoin mining return of $15,000,000 if we multiply that by a hypothetical exchange rate of 1 Bitcoin to $8,500.

Let's use the cloud mining platform Hashtoro.com to compute our profit. If you spend 3.000 euros on an annual contract for 75 TH, you may be confident that you will have made almost 1.7 bitcoin after all running costs are paid. That doesn't even consider the appreciation effect of a rising crypto market.

While there is a range of crypto investments to pick from, the most are 'high risk, high reward' in nature, meaning you might make a huge profit as well as a crash to the ground.

However, if you want to invest in cryptocurrencies as a legal source of continuous, passive income, you should use cloud mining businesses' services.

AUTOMATE YOUR SAVINGS

Passive income is one of the wealth-building and wealth-maintenance tactics. At least seven separate revenue streams are used by the average millionaire, with at least half of them being passive. This suggests that HNIs aren't aggressively exchanging their time for money. They are putting their money to work for them instead.

The crypto industry can offer far more lucrative opportunities than the traditional system for people with cash to put their money to work for them and earn a passive income alongside their active income. Passive income is a type of revenue that does not involve any engagement or time-consuming work to generate a profit. Don't be alarmed the next time you hear about

Bitcoins, Litecoins, Dodgecoins, and other digital currencies and the profit potential; this is simply part of the new era of digital currencies and a more computerized world. Without a doubt, everything is going virtual. Writing and mailing used to be the only means of communication. Writing and emailing are the primary modes of communication today. The sole difference is the addition of an "e," as in electronic.

Money is no different. We began using salt, meals, and precious metals as money, progressing to coins, paper, and virtual money. Credit cards, debit cards, e-checks, ACH, and other virtual money are now widely used. Money earned by your things without participation is referred to as passive income. Profits from a rental property, evergreen automatic sales for a company, dividends from stock holdings, or any other type of income could be included. Another source of passive income is interest earned on bank accounts and, more recently, cryptocurrency holdings. Any investment that generates income on its own is considered passive.

Thousands of people invest in bitcoin to supplement their income, but cryptocurrency investment is not the same as passive income. Cryptocurrency investing is difficult. It necessitates trend analysis and nerve-wracking decisions on when to sell up. Aside from market gains or losses, there's not a lot that's passive about bitcoin investments.

Cryptocurrencies, like traditional currencies, can generate interest when maintained in a savings account. They can also be deposited to other platforms to earn a return. Some of these are centralized cryptocurrency savings accounts, such as those offered by Nexo, BlockFi, and Crypto.com, which use your funds to provide institutional borrowers with overcollateralized loans. Similarly, many exchanges, including Binance and Huobi, offer users a return on their cryptocurrency deposits.

Others, such as Orion Money and Anchor, are decentralized savings services that allow you to earn interest on your stablecoin investments. Yearn Finance and Autofarm, for example, will automatically move your funds amongst a variety of DeFi products to maximize your yield.

Because they require little to no in-depth understanding to get started, these are undoubtedly the simplest and most basic strategies to generate a passive dividend on your bitcoin deposits.

How much money can you make?

It's normally feasible to earn 5-20% APY depending on the asset you stake and the platform you choose.

What should you be wary of?

Be aware of platforms that appear to provide suspiciously large rewards; they could be Ponzi schemes.

Earning interest.

Tokens are deposited into a crypto "bank" account. The financial institution lends the cryptocurrency and pays interest to the depositors in exchange.

Why Is Interest An Important Part Of Crypto Investors' Passive Income?

Crypto investments can now earn passive income through centralized finance (CeFi) institutions. This is accomplished by paying interest on deposits stored at the institution.

Earning interest on cryptocurrency holdings is similar to earning interest on fiat currencies. When you deposit money (in US dollars) into a high-yield savings account at a bank, you can expect to receive an interest of roughly 1% every year. Your money is put to good use by the bank, which lends it to qualified borrowers. On the money you earn, you earn a tiny bit of interest. The bank also profiteers from the spread.

The cryptocurrency analogues of banks are CeFi entities. They are not protected in the same way banks are (aka, you could lose your crypto tokens due to theft). They do, however, serve a comparable purpose. A CeFi institution like Hodlnaut accepts cryptocurrency deposits. It lends such tokens to creditworthy individuals and businesses. The bank then pays interest to depositors. The interest is usually paid in the same token that was lent out. However, some companies allow depositors to select their preferred interest token.

And the danger appears to be high. Cryptocurrency interest rates are currently exorbitant compared to interest rates on conventional currencies. On the other hand, many bitcoin investors are still hesitant to deposit their funds with CeFi facilities. Crypto "banking" is still a new notion, despite many organizations having asset protection insurance plans.

CeFi institutions, on the other hand, generally pay investors well for taking on that risk. Hodlnaut, for example, is currently giving up to 12.73 percent APY on your deposits. That's a solid return for merely maintaining your money in an account.

Why Is Earning Interest On Crypto Holdings So Important?

Many cryptocurrency owners have seen significant increases in the value of their tokens over the last few years. Bitcoin was valued at less than $1 in 2011. The coin now has a worth of over $47,000. With the tremendous increase in value, the easiest approach to acquire value in digital currencies may be to "buy and hold."

One Bitcoin, however, was worth one Bitcoin in 2011 and is still worth one Bitcoin today. While the monetary value has increased tremendously, the underlying asset has remained the same. Digital currencies, in this sense, do not "increase in value" in the same way that most traditional investments (such as equities, ETFs, bonds, and even real estate) do. Compounding growth is a feature of all traditional investments (compounding interest or increasing value over time).

The value of a digital token is solely determined by demand unless it earns interest. The demand for digital tokens has grown at an exponential rate since 2011. However, there is no certainty that the current expansion rate will continue.

Earning interest in digital currency ensures that the asset's underlying worth grows over time. For example, if you have 1 Bitcoin today and earn interest at Hodlnaut, you can anticipate having 1.06 Bitcoin after a year. When you earn interest on a token, regardless of the current trade price for Bitcoin, you possess more of it. You're boosting the underlying worth of your investment by generating interest.

How to Find a Cryptocurrency Account That Pays Passive Income

When it comes to putting tokens on deposit, cryptocurrency investors who aren't used to working with CeFi institutions may be apprehensive. The apprehension is understandable.

Scam companies acting as CeFi institutions might defraud investors of their money. In addition, hackers attempting to steal digital currency are targeting CeFi institutions. To reduce the danger of putting tokens on deposit, you should first research the platform and the company.

PARTICIPATE IN A YIELD FARM

Yield farming is another way to make a passive crypto income that is decentralized or Defi. The dynamic operations of decentralized exchanges, which are essentially trading platforms where users rely on a combination of smart contracts (programmable and self-executing computer contracts) and investors for the liquidity required to execute trades, make this possible. Users do not compete with brokers or other traders on this platform. Instead, they trade against cash put in special smart contracts known as liquidity pools by investors (known as liquidity providers). Liquidity providers, in turn, receive a proportional share of the pool's trading fees.

You must first become a liquidity provider (LP) on a DeFi exchange such as Uniswap, Aave, or PancakeSwap to begin earning passive money through this mechanism. To begin earning these fees, you must deposit a certain ratio of two or more digital assets into a liquidity pool.

To offer liquidity to an ETH/USDT pool, for example, you must deposit both ETH and USDT tokens into it. Once you've deposited liquidity, the decentralized exchange will provide you LP tokens, representing your portion of the total funds in the liquidity pool. You can then use supported decentralized lending platforms to stake these LP tokens and earn additional interest. With this method, you can earn two different interest rates on a single deposit.

It's important to note that none of these chances is without risk. The crypto passive income options described here are only a few of the various ways you can profit from your idle digital assets. As a result, it's a good idea to do your study, seek expert advice from a certified financial advisor, and figure out what best meets your investing objectives.

LIQUIDITY HARVESTING OR YIELD FARMING

Yield farming is a method of increasing the value of your crypto assets by lending them to DeFi lending sites. You can earn fees and tokens in exchange for supplying cash to develop the liquidity pools on these platforms, based on your portion of the liquidity pool.

All you have to do is send a particular amount of Cryptocurrency (typically a large amount) to a DeFi platform like Uniswap or Aave. You deposit Crypto into a particular liquidity pool in a predetermined ratio of crypto pairs (such as ETH/USD).

The funds will be placed in a liquidity pool, and you will be given LP (Liquidity Provider) tokens in exchange for your portion of the pool's total funds, which will earn you interest over time. You can then use these tokens to generate extra income on your Crypto by staking them on DeFi platforms. **Does it appear to be difficult?**

Yield farming is a lot easier to do in practice, but it's also a lot riskier. As the liquidity pool grows in popularity, your locked crypto assets could be stolen (scammed), hacked, decline in value (permanent loss), or earn very little income.

Provider of Liquidity (LP)

By depositing equivalent USD quantities of a trading pair to a smart contract, investors with capital can earn passive income in the form of interest fees and other rewards for supplying liquidity to borrowing and lending platforms. Liquidity providers are compensated with transaction fees when they supply liquidity to a platform. The most prominent decentralized cryptocurrency exchange, Uniswap, is a platform that allows for the provision of liquidity in DeFi (Decentralized Finance).

DIVIDEND-EARNING TOKENS

Money earned from ventures in which an individual is not actively involved is passive income. Earnings are stable and predictable in some circumstances. In other cases, factors beyond your control may play a role. Most of the time, all you have to do is put your money or digital assets into a certain Crypto investing plan or platform and wait for it to make money.

Buying and holding Crypto, often known as "HODLing" in the market, is a common technique for people to get a return in Crypto with little to no engagement. This means that an investor is willing to buy a digital asset with the expectation that its value will rise dramatically in the future. These investors are willing to go the extra mile, as this long-term approach may require them to maintain their assets for up to five years. An investor does not need to be engaged in the crypto market for the duration of this investment. They only need to purchase the digital asset and deposit it in a safe wallet, preferably not under their control.

A wallet is a device or program that stores a private key to access your Cryptocurrency. The non-custodial varieties let you keep the private key on your devices, such as a computer, a phone, or a wallet. You'll have complete control over your private keys and, ultimately, your digital assets if you do it this way. On the other hand, your private keys are controlled by a third party in a custodial wallet.

However, purchasing and holding a crypto asset for an extended period does not guarantee a profit. There's a good chance you'll lose money. As a result, HODLing crypto solely cannot be regarded a true passive income producer.

Certain tokens provide holders with a portion of the revenue generated by the company that created them. You are automatically entitled to get a specific amount of the company's revenue if you only hold the token. The percentage of revenue you earn is determined by the number of tokens you own. KuCoin Shares (KCS) are an example of this, with investors receiving a daily part of the KuCoin blockchain asset exchange's transaction fees. The amount paid is proportional to each holder's number of KCS tokens staked.

DIVIDENDS ON TOKENS CAN BE EARNED.

Holding dividend-paying tokens is perhaps one of the most straightforward ways to make passive income in Crypto. These tokens are issued by crypto platforms such as exchanges and DeFi institutions, much like shares in a company.

Users that acquire and hold these tokens will receive dividends, and the more tokens you retain, the more dividends you will receive.

One of the best instances of dividend-paying tokens is KuCoin Shares (KCS). On the largest crypto exchange, KuCoin, KCS tokens can receive dividends. The value of the KCS tokens increases as the exchange expands, much like the value of a cryptocurrency.

Another cryptocurrency company that pays out 80 percent of its income as dividends are the Celsius Network DeFi platform. Bibox Tokens (BIX) is a third example, which returns 45 percent of Bibox's net trading fee revenues to its "shareholders."

DIVIDEND-PAYING CRYPTOCURRENCIES

Staking, holding, and running master nodes will provide an ideal opportunity to get your hands on some of these cheap coins and make smart passive income through regular dividends.

Typically, people believe that day-trading is the only way to make money in Crypto. I, on the other hand, respectfully disagree. There are hundreds of other smart methods to gain in the crypto sphere.

Since I initially purchased Bitcoin and Ethereum, I experimented with these methods. I've also become addicted to this environment since then, and I've accumulated useful knowledge and tips to make my adventure even more fascinating.

However, before I tell you about the cryptos that pay dividends in the form of smart passive income, let me explain what dividends are and how you might earn them.

WHAT ARE CRYPTO DIVIDENDS, AND HOW DO THEY WORK?

A dividend is a distribution of a portion of a company's earnings to a class of shareholders set by the board of directors. Dividends can be paid in cash, like stock shares or other property.

Crypto dividends refer to a similar notion of profit-sharing used by several cryptocurrency companies. Remember that this is not the same as airdrops, which are essentially diluting total supply, resulting in diluting everyone's holdings.

Dividends Can Be Earned in a Variety of Ways in Crypto

You can receive dividends in the crypto world in various ways by HOLDING a cryptocurrency. These, on the other hand, differ from currency to currency because each has its own set of rules and regulations.

The following are some of the most popular ways to earn dividends:

Holding Proof-of-Stake coins in a specific wallet or supported exchange is staking. Indeed, you should begin with these proof-of-stake cryptocurrencies, similar to dividends.

HOLDING– Purchasing a cryptocurrency and storing it in a wallet.

Based on these various categories, I've compiled a list of cryptocurrencies that I believe are worth holding for their bright future and the opportunity to receive passive income in the form of dividends.

List of Cryptocurrencies That Pay Dividends To Earn Passive Income

Buying and holding dividend-paying tokens is another way to make passive income in the cryptocurrency market. Despite their rarity, exchange-issued tokens are the most popular digital tokens that pay dividends. Several digital asset exchanges have launched their tokens, which offer customers reduced trading fees and, in some circumstances, a portion of the platform's revenues.

To get dividends on these tokens, holders must keep them on the issuing exchange or stake them using an external wallet. The more tokens you own, the more passive revenue you'll be able to generate. KuCoin (KCS) and Bibox are two exchange tokens that pay a dividend (BIX).

1. **Looks:** Looks is a new cryptocurrency introduced by the NFT marketplace LooksRare. The platform distributes the ethereum it earns (from NFT transaction fees) to Looks token holders. You will receive WETH dividends by staking the $Looks token on the Looksrare staking page (Wrapped ethereum). This project was begun in January 2022, and it's something you should keep an eye on.

The $Looks token is available on the following exchanges:

Huobi

- Global
- Bybit
- FTX
- Uniswap

Withdraw the $Looks token from your dAPP crypto wallets, such as Metamask or Trustwallet, once you've purchased it. Then go to Looksrare.org/rewards and stake your $Looks token there.

You can also check out the current staking rewards.

2. Komodo

Komodo is a prominent cryptocurrency with an improved consensus method and anonymity features. It is also a pioneer in designing an atomic swap enabled P2P decentralized exchange called BarterDex, part of a larger decentralized economy system called SuperNET. KMD pays for simply responsibly holding its currency.

However, it is not like pure staking, where you must keep your wallet open at all times. Instead, keep your KMD in a wallet and rotate it every year.

Binance wallet – Staking wallet

Purchase Komodo Now

Login to your Binance account (or create one if you don't have one) once you have the KMD token.

To deposit, go to Earn > Staking Search for Komodo and then click Deposit.

You can start receiving dividends for your Komodo holdings by following the guidelines.

3. Ascendex

Ascendex is a new exchange with its native coin, ASD. The price of an ASD token is only 25 cents at writing, yet demand for this coin is growing. What's more, ASD allows you to receive a part of the exchange income. Once you've purchased the ASD token, you can lock it up using this exchange's locking feature (you can withdraw at any moment, but it will take 24 hours), and you'll start earning USDT.

To do so, go to the "assets" page and select "request for lock-up" after purchasing the BTMX coin. Every day, the prize is calculated and distributed. This is one of the greatest crypto dividends currencies you can buy.

4. KuCoin

KuCoin is a world-class blockchain asset exchange that debuted in mid-2017 and has seen significant growth in 2018 due to its business model and marketing efforts. They have their native token, KuCoin shares, just like Binance, but their mechanism for rewarding its holders is different, which I enjoy.

You get a daily bonus/dividend called KuCoin Bonus if you keep these KuCoin shares. You will receive a bonus equal to 50% of your trading fees. As a result, if the volume and number of coins traded on the KuCoin exchange increases, the benefit of owning KuCoin Shares will increase as well.

Note that KuCoin has a history of modifying its policies. As a result, you should double-check before using the KCS token's dividend-paying feature.

Annual Return – KCS Ticker Symbol – Varies depending on exchange trade volume

5. NEO

NEO is a prominent cryptocurrency that is also known as Chinese Ethereum.

On NEO's blockchain, there is also a coin called NEO. Apart from the NEO cryptocurrency, NEO also features a crypto-token known as GAS (previously known as ANC or Antcoins) that may be staked in a NEO wallet for a profit. In addition, unlike other POS cryptos, it does not require you to keep your staking wallets open at all times.

But keep in mind that only a few wallets allow you to claim the GAS, so you'll need to choose the proper wallet to receive the GAS as dividends.

One receives a return in the form of NeoGAS, which is presently worth $44.5 per unit.

NEO Annual Return – 5.5 percent

6. Neblio

Neblio is a relatively new player in this market. It's a blockchain platform for building decentralized apps, smart contracts, and ICOs.

However, it is currently gaining popularity due to its development plan and standard examples of implementing it.

You might argue it's a competitor to Ethereum, NEO, and Qtum's blockchains, but I don't believe it's a zero-sum game. I believe Neblio blockchain will carve its niche among organizations, just like other blockchain-as-a-service platforms.

The native currency of this proof of stake blockchain, the 'Nebl,' can be staked in their official wallet and on a Raspberry Pi to yield a nice 10% yearly return on total holdings.

7. PIVX

PIVX is another proof-of-stake currency that uses the Zerocoin system to remain anonymous. PIVX: Everything You Need To Know is a good place to learn about Cryptocurrency. It also offers a staking model, similar to practically all proof-of-stake currencies, that pays well for staking and keeping your PIVX tokens in a wallet. Furthermore, there is no staking limit.

However, the wallets must be open and online to claim the staking benefits for a specified period.

8. NAVCoin

It is a fully working point-of-sale cryptocurrency that has been in operation since 2014 and is based on the Bitcoin core code. Faster transactions (30 seconds), configurable privacy with multiple blockchains, and a POS staking rewards structure that allows you to earn while you sleep are just a few of the benefits of this currency. There is also no staking limit.

NAV Annual Return - Up to 5%

BITCOIN INVESTMENT AND TRADING BOT

Bitcoins and other cryptocurrencies have become an unavoidable aspect of modern life. Our race's evolution has led us to a more convenient method of exchanging money: digital money.

The first thing that comes to mind for someone unfamiliar with Bitcoin is, "What is Bitcoin?" Another topic that is frequently asked is the Bitcoin price.

When it was first introduced in early 2009, it cost less than ten cents per Bitcoin. Since then, it has consistently grown, lately hovering around $4000 per Bitcoin. So, in terms of Bitcoin value or Bitcoin rate, this has been a phenomenal increase in value, resulting in the creation of many, many millionaires over the last eight years.

The Bitcoin market is global, and China, Japan, and other Asian countries have been particularly active purchasing it. The Bitcoin history graph is fascinating. It was created by an anonymous group of clever mathematicians (using the pseudonym Satoski Nakamoto) in 2008 as "virtual gold," The initial Bitcoin software was launched in early 2009 amid the US economic crisis. They understood that, like gold, it had to have a finite quantity to have permanent value. As a result, they set a limit of 21 million Bitcoins when they created it.

CRYPTOCURRENCY TRADING BOTS: WHAT YOU SHOULD KNOW

In an era where bots appear to be used practically everywhere, it's no wonder that they've made their way into bitcoin trading.

Let's learn more about these bots and explain some essential points.

Trading bots for a cryptocurrency (or crypto) are computer programs that allow you to acquire and sell coins at the optimal time. They want to make money for their customers and give them a competitive advantage in the long run. The bots keep a close eye on market conditions and make transactions based on pre-defined algorithms. It's also worth mentioning that you're allowed to specify your parameters, which will aid in the execution of numerous deals. Because this type of software can answer approximately a thousand times faster than a human, its operational efficiency is unthinkable.

There are numerous sorts of cryptocurrency trading bots. Trend-following bots, arbitrage bots, and scalping bots are among them. Arbitrage bots, however, are the most popular, according to bitcoin.com.

Trend bots are useful if you're primarily interested in trends while developing your plans. These algorithms can spot trends and determine whether it's a good time to buy or sell something.

Scalping programs make it easier for consumers to perform better in sideways markets. This implies that scalpers,' as these users are commonly known, can purchase something at a low price and then resell it for a higher discount price.

On the other hand, Arbitrage bots are designed to make money by comparing prices across several exchanges and exploiting price differences.

If you've decided to put cryptocurrency trading bots to use in your firm, you need to consider which one will meet your needs. Keep in mind that each bot has different software and hardware requirements. Before making a decision, think about everything.

After all of the procedures are taken care of, you can begin the installation process. You can get a trading bot by using one of the three methods listed below:

- It's available for free on an open-source platform;
- Purchase a licensed bot's paying version;
- Make a trading robot (if you possess enough technical knowledge and skills).

After going through all of the information above, you've most likely formed an opinion regarding crypto trading bots. Still, let's go over all of their benefits over humans.

- Bots are unquestionably a hundred times faster than humans.
- Stamina: bots can work nonstop 24 hours a day, seven days a week.
- Bots can process gigabytes of data each second.
- Bots have no emotions of any kind; thus, they are completely objective. They merely carry out their responsibilities.

Many scientists, however, argue that in some circumstances, subjective reasoning is required and that humans can beat soulless robots in this way. However, because bots provide so many incredible chances, you'll almost certainly be better off once you give them top priority.

As you can see, bitcoin trading bots are quite useful and versatile, allowing you to make money. Just keep in mind that scrutinizing bots' specifics is highly suggested if you want to give them complete playtime. Then you stand a good chance of benefiting from this brilliant technology.

When Choosing A Bitcoin Trading Bot, Keep These Things in Mind

The cryptocurrency market has grown in popularity, and every trader wants to make a fortune with bitcoin trading. It is, however, an extremely volatile market that can be difficult to keep up with, especially because, unlike the stock market, it is a market that never sleeps. Trading bots have been developed to make things easier for traders. A trading bot is a software program designed to communicate directly with financial exchanges to gather and interpret pertinent information to purchase and sell orders on the traders' behalf.

If you're new to bitcoin trading, you might want to look for the finest bitcoin trading bot to help you get started. The bot evaluates market actions such as price, volume, and orders and judgments based on your interests and tastes as a trader. In essence, the bots make decisions based on market price movement and pre-programmed rules to avoid losses. But how do you know which bot is the best when there are so many?

Customization and user-friendliness

A decent trading bot's interface should be simple to use for any trader, including those who aren't familiar with coding. All relevant information should be easily accessible, and profits should be readily displayed, along with all aspects of trading that matter, such as buy orders and current sales. All you should have to do is enter your pairs and numbers and start trading with a single click. A customisable trading bot is much better, as it is easy to use even for first-time users. You will be able to change the appearance of the skin with this function, resulting in an application that you will like using every time.

Compatibility with various operating systems

Not all bots are created equal, and not every trader uses the same operating system. As a result, you'll want to purchase a platform that works across all operating systems. Depending on the system you're using, you may access your trades using a bot like this from Linux, Mac, or Windows. With your orders and settings on a USB, all you have to do is connect it to any computer to continue trading, regardless of the operating system. In the end, a standalone bot that does not require installation and is compatible with all operating systems will be highly useful.

Pairs, cryptocurrencies, and exchanges are all supported.

Besides bitcoin, you could be a trader interested in other pairs, exchanges, and coins. Finding a trader bot that can handle multiple coins supplied by major exchanges might thus be more beneficial. A full-featured crypto bot will be ideal for a trader that trades on the spur of the moment.

Notifications and reporting and real-time and historical backtesting are additional bot functions that could be useful. Find out what the trading bot can accomplish and make the appropriate choice.

A bitcoin trading bot can eliminate the guesswork in the trading process. There are numerous bots available, and your task should be to select the best bitcoin trading bot to have a rewarding trading experience.

INVESTING

A common concern is the possibility of a Bitcoin scam. A friend bought something from a corporation that claimed 1% to 2% daily growth. My friend lost all of the money he had invested, which was several thousand dollars, because the company's website had no contact information. After a few months, the website mysteriously vanished one day.

To get started, one must first learn how to buy Bitcoins, purchase Bitcoin, and buy Bitcoin with a credit card. Coinbase is a well-known platform for doing so. Their commission is 3.75 percent, with a daily purchase limit of $10,000. This would most likely be the simplest method of purchasing bitcoins.

Others would want to purchase Bitcoin with a debit card. Coinbase offers this service as well, with explicit step-by-step instructions on how to use your debit or credit card.

Some people want to purchase Bitcoin right now. This can be done using W. Union or any credit/debit card at Paxful, Inc.

Other often asked topics include the best way to acquire Bitcoins, get Bitcoins, and buy Bitcoins online. This is almost certainly the best location to get Bitcoins. The most straightforward method is to purchase it through a digital asset exchange, such as Coinbase. It's simple to open an account with them, and once you've linked your bank account, you can effortlessly purchase and trade Bitcoin.

Understanding what a Bitcoin wallet is and how to utilize it is necessary. It's nothing more than a Bitcoin version of a bank account. It enables you to receive, store, and send Bitcoins to others. Its function is to keep a set of Bitcoin privacy keys. It is usually password-protected or otherwise secured from unauthorized access.

There are various types of digital wallets available. You may send, receive, and store Bitcoin using your web browser with a web wallet. On the other hand, a desktop wallet is one in which the wallet software is installed directly on your computer. Mobile wallets are wallets that are designed to be used on a mobile device.

The topic of Bitcoin stock, or how to buy Bitcoin stock, comes up now and then. Buying Bitcoin directly, rather than its stock, is the most usual approach to proceed in this area.

A Bitcoin Investment Trust is an investment fund to track the Bitcoin market movement. Some analysts, however, believe that this is a hazardous approach to enter the market.

What is the best way for me to invest?

First, you must make an account with a trading platform and create a wallet; examples may be found by searching Google for 'Bitcoin trading platform' they usually have titles that include the words 'coin' or market.' After joining one of these platforms, you select your currency by clicking on assets, then crypto. There are several vital signs on every platform, and you should be sure to pay attention to them before investing.

Simply purchase and hold.

While mining is the safest and, in some ways, the simplest way to earn Bitcoin, it requires much too much effort, and the cost of power and specialized computer hardware makes it prohibitively expensive for most of us. To avoid all of this, make it simple for yourself by immediately entering the amount you want from your bank and clicking "purchase," then sitting back and seeing your investment grow in line with the price change. This is known as an exchange, and it takes place on many of today's exchange platforms, which allow you to trade between a variety of fiat currencies

(USD, AUD, GBP, etc.) and crypto coins (Bitcoin, Ethereum, Litecoin, etc.).

YOUR BITCOIN INVESTING STRATEGY

If you want to invest in Bitcoin, you should think about many things. You don't want to put your hard-earned cash in jeopardy. Rather, every investor's purpose is to maximize the return on their investment dollars. This conclusion should be based on a thorough technical investigation and review.

Let's look at a few pointers to help you improve your investment approach.

1. Understand the Fundamentals

The first stage ensures that you can profit from your investment, which you can only do if you understand the fundamentals. If you don't fully grasp the principles, you may find yourself making poor decisions.

To mention a few words, you should be familiar with cryptocurrency trading, private keys, public keys, wallets, and digital coins. It is critical to understand this fundamental terminology to make better financial selections.

2. Maintain Consistency

For various reasons, we frequently wait too long to make crucial judgments. In reality, even seasoned investors are susceptible to making this error. It's critical to recognize the need of adjusting your plans in response to market conditions. Because the value of Bitcoin fluctuates, you'll need to adjust your investment methods from time to time.

3. Make use of technology

Because the digital currency notion is based on technology, you should select your investment. You can, for example, use automated bots to assist with cryptocurrency trading. As a result, you won't need to intercede as much.

This type of software can help you save time and effort while making decisions. As a result, employing them is a brilliant idea.

4. Take Exchange Rates into Account

When choosing a cryptocurrency exchange, you need to be very picky. Various exchanges have different tariff rates, which might significantly impact your return on investment. This is significant if you do a lot of tiny trades because each transaction is charged according to the exchange's laws and regulations. As a result, you should make sure that you choose the finest exchange to save money.

5. Don't Excessively Trade

Some investors tend to overtrade at the beginning. They make multiple deals per day, which is a huge mistake. You should probably avoid it because the consequences can be disastrous. As a result, you should take your time and consider each trading decision carefully.

6. Think about other options

Your BTC investment could be highly profitable in some cases. You could choose to go with an option that reduces your risk while increasing your return. As a result, you should choose a low-risk, higher-profit choice.

To cut a long tale short, investing in BTC can be very profitable, especially if you take it slowly and carefully. So, to make the greatest pick, make sure you study the fundamentals and analyze different options. I hope this information is useful.

WHY SHOULD YOU PUT YOUR MONEY INTO BITCOIN?

As you can see, investing in Bitcoin necessitates a fundamental understanding of the currency, as described above. It entails risk, just like any other investment! The decision to invest or not depends totally on the person. However, if I were to give advice, I would recommend investing in Bitcoin since it continues to grow - despite one huge boom and bust period, it is quite likely that Cryptocurrencies as a whole will continue to gain in value over the next ten years. Bitcoin is the most popular and well-known of all current cryptocurrencies, so it's a smart place to start and currently the safest bet. Although Bitcoin trading is risky in the near term, I believe you will find it more successful than most other investments.

Bitcoin's Advantages

1. Sending Money Is Simple

Because it is decentralized, you can send Bitcoin (money) to a buddy on the opposite side of the planet in seconds without going through a financial intermediary (and paying the banking fees).

Bitcoin's popularity is based solely on this fact. Rather than waiting days for a wire transfer, you can send your payment in seconds or minutes.

2. Limited Quantity

The total number of Bitcoins that will ever be mined is limited to 21 million. This restricts the total amount of Bitcoin that can ever be created. This is the same as stating a government can't issue money because the supply of banknotes is limited - and they won't print anymore.

Your purchasing power is conserved, and the currency is immune to rapid inflation when there is a fixed supply.

This limited supply has also aided in the growth in Bitcoin's price. People do not want a currency created - or inflated - indefinitely by a selfish government.

3. Private

The majority of people believe Bitcoin is entirely anonymous. However, it is not anonymous; rather, it is more private. The Blockchain - the public Bitcoin ledger - contains a record of all Bitcoin transactions ever made.

Each transaction is associated with an address, a text and a character string.

However, the transaction's name and identifying information are not visible. People may see your address, but they will not link it to you.

Many consumers like this privacy feature because they don't want their banks snooping on them (or telling them how much of their own money they can or can't transfer).

4. Transactions are less expensive

To stay competitive, many establishments now accept Visa or MasterCard. On the other hand, these cards deduct a significant amount of money from each sale.

A merchant who accepts Bitcoin, on the other hand, does not have to pay these exorbitant fees, putting more money in their pocket.

So those are some of the most important advantages of Bitcoins. What about the disadvantages?

Bitcoin's drawbacks

1. Dangerous: Price Fluctuations

Bitcoin is known for increasing steadily over months, then plummeting by 20 to 50 percent in a matter of days.

The price is always fluctuating because it is traded 24 hours a day, seven days a week. And all it takes is a single piece of bad news, such as the revelation of the Mt Gox breach a few years ago, to send the price plummeting.

So, in a nutshell, it's not steady, and there are a lot of unknowns that can influence the price. The golden rule is never to invest money in Bitcoin that you cannot afford to lose.

2. Transaction Speeds Should Be Slowed

Slower transaction speeds and increased transaction fees are causing challenges for Bitcoin. Other cryptocurrencies have emerged that are both speedier and less expensive.

Bitcoin miners are working on the problem. However, you may expect the price to be extremely erratic until these flaws are fixed.

3. Reversible Bitcoin Transactions

Bitcoin transactions, unlike credit card charges, are irreversible. As a result, if you send Bitcoin to the wrong address, you will not retrieve it.

There are also several accounts of people who have lost their Bitcoin wallet addresses (due to hacking, phone theft, virus-infected computers, and so on) and have fully lost their funds. It's impossible to get them back.

As a result, if you want to invest in Bitcoins - or any other cryptocurrency you need to know what you're doing and take the time to understand how to buy and manage your coins properly.

While Bitcoin has many positive attributes and can revolutionize financial transactions as we know them, there are still many risks involved. There are still a lot of unknowns in the world. So those are a few things to think about before investing in Bitcoin.

Take your time and investigate your options if you do decide to buy. Don't just buy from any merchant. Some of them are reliable and run successful businesses. On the other hand, others may overcharge you and may even fail to deliver your coins.

Be cautious and do your homework first. Find a reputable seller with a good track record - there are plenty of them out there. Also, keep in mind the golden rule: never invest more money than you can afford to lose.

MINING

The process of creating new Bitcoins is known as bitcoin mining. The government decides when and where to print and distribute traditional cash. Bitcoin "miners" employ specialized software to solve difficult mathematical problems in exchange for a set quantity of Bitcoins.

The question then becomes whether Bitcoin mining is worthwhile. For the average person, the answer is no. It necessitates extremely advanced knowledge and a strong computer system, and this combination of features renders it inaccessible to the general public. This holds for bitcoin mining in 2017, much more than in previous years.

Bitcoin Mining for Beginners: A Step-by-Step Guide

The act of confirming transactions on each Blockchain is known as Bitcoin mining. Bitcoin miners are in charge of verifying and validating each transaction before adding to a block to construct a blockchain. Every transaction is then given validity, and the transaction is then shared publicly over the peer-to-peer network for all to view. When miners add the next block to the blockchain, they are eligible for a payout, usually in bitcoins. The higher the reward, the more mathematical calculations you solve.

To participate in Bitcoin mining, you do not need to be a skilled software engineer or coder. A step-by-step guide for Bitcoin mining beginners is provided below.

Get yourself some Bitcoin mining hardware.

Bitcoin mining equipment

As more computer power is used in mining, the world of mining becomes increasingly complex. Because the investment in gear is so significant, the higher the mining level, the more difficult it is to profit. Bitcoin mining is a very competitive industry; therefore, you should do your homework before investing in hardware. Previously, you could mine Bitcoins with your home computer's CPU; however, this method is no longer practical due to the intricacy of mining. You'll need to invest in a custom-built computer that's sole function is bitcoin mining.

Get yourself a Bitcoin wallet.

Wallet for Bitcoin

To keep your digital currency, you'll need a wallet, which might be local or online. The most critical things to remember about a wallet are the Public Wallet Address and the private key or password. To protect your investment if your wallet is self-hosted, you'll need a copy of the wallat.dat file. It serves as a backup wallet if something goes wrong with your machine. Wallets for mobile devices are also available. The self-hosted or locally created wallet is strongly recommended.

Look for a pool to join.

Pool of Mining

Mining is difficult, and you may never see a return on your investment. It is suggested that you join a mining pool or mine alone. A mining pool is a collection of miners who join forces to share resources and rewards. A pool ensures faster returns because your processing power is pooled for better outcomes. Each pool has its own rules, reward mechanism, and mining fee. You must choose one that best meets your requirements.

For your computer, get mining software.

Pool of Mining

Depending on the gear you have, there are a variety of free mining apps. The mining software aids in the monitoring and control of your devices. CGminer, BFGminer, and EasyMiner are three popular mining applications. You should contact them before linking your pool to your program if you have a pool. The programs run from a command line and may require a batch file to get started.

Mine

After that, you're good to go. Start your mining program by entering the username and password for your pool. As the miner works, you'll notice that your machine slows down.

Because the program causes your hardware to heat up, it's critical to keep an eye on the temperatures. Some programs, such as SpeedFan, can regulate the temperature. After a while, you should evaluate your earnings to see if your investment is still worthwhile. You don't want to risk losing all of your money before you even begin working.

ACCEPTING BITCOIN AS A PAYMENT

Many people are curious as to who takes Bitcoin. What are some stores that accept bitcoin, what are some websites that accept bitcoins, what are some retailers that accept bitcoin, what are some places that accept bitcoin, and where can I spend bitcoin questions that people ask?

Accepting cryptocurrency as a legal payment option is becoming increasingly popular among businesses. The main corporations are DISH Network, Microsoft, Expedia, Shopify stores, Newegg, Payza, 2Pay4You, and others. Walmart and Amazon are two prominent holdouts at the moment.

Ethereum is the strongest competitor to Bitcoin in the cryptocurrency industry, and many people are curious about the Bitcoin vs Ethereum debate. Ethereum was launched in mid-2015 and has garnered considerable traction, but it still trails Bitcoin in terms of usage, acceptance, and value.

Bitcoin's current exchange rate

Since its debut in the global financial marketplace, the USD has been a carefully observed benchmark daily and long-term. XE is a popular firm for getting the most up-to-date Bitcoin valuation. They display the Bitcoin to the

USD exchange rate and the entire Bitcoin price chart, Bitcoin value chart, and Bitcoin to USD chart. If you ask, "How much is one Bitcoin?" their constantly updated charts will always tell you.

AFFILIATE EARNINGS

Bitwol is one company that allows you to convert Bitcoin to Bitcoin cash, i.e. receive USD by selling Bitcoin. Another firm that will walk you through this procedure is WikiHow.

Bitcoin as a Stock

Other companies allow you to acquire shares in companies that invest in Bitcoin; these companies handle the back-and-forth trading, and you simply invest and wait for your monthly advantages. These firms simply pool digital funds from various sources and invest on their behalf.

BITCOIN TRADING

If you're familiar with stocks, bonds, or currency exchanges, you'll have no trouble understanding crypto-trading. You can choose from Bitcoin brokers such as e-social trading, FXTM markets.com, and many others. The platforms offer Bitcoin-fiat and fiat-Bitcoin currency pairs, such as BTCUSD, which allows you to trade Bitcoins for US Dollars. Keep an eye on price changes to locate the ideal pair based on price changes; systems provide pricing, among other indications, to provide you with appropriate trading advice.

MICRO EARNINGS

Bitcoin is the world's first peer-to-peer crypto-currency that isn't regulated by a central authority and is an open-source protocol that all participants in the economy obey. The supply of Bitcoins cannot be manipulated, and all transactions in this currency are cryptographically confirmed through a process known as Bitcoin mining. Your Bitcoins are secure to the best of public-key cryptography's ability.

Bitcoin is at the top of the mountain on new year's eve. The dark days appear to be behind us, and while a bitcoin bubble could erupt at any time, there is no doubt that bitcoin is here to stay. The sooner you start making money with bitcoin, the better off you'll be in five years when it becomes a globally accepted currency.

If you're worried about the Bubble, investing in bitcoin is one choice, but it's not the only one. Bitcoin, bubble or not, can still make you a lot of money. And, bubble or not, the value will continue to climb in the future since more individuals are becoming interested.

After you've grasped the fundamentals of Bitcoin, the next obvious question is: how can you get any Bitcoin? Here are some suggestions:

1. Make money online and exchange it for Bitcoin.

It is still much easier to make US Dollars, believe it or not! If you're in the United States, you may then convert your dollars for Bitcoin at any of the exchanges, such as Bitstamp or Coinbase.

In the Bitcoin economy, you can earn Bitcoin directly.

There is a tiny yet active community where you may complete most jobs in a smaller size. For example, on Coinality, you can get a part-time job for Bitcoin, or on Coingig, you can get a modest gig. In the Bitcoin ecosystem, these are the real-life equivalents of sites like Elance and Fiverr.

2. Advertising

Not unexpectedly, the Bitcoin economy's advertising industry is thriving. This is due to the constant emergence of new Bitcoin-based services requiring a robust advertising network.

Other services, such as Bitads, allow advertisers to bid for banner space on your blog, while CoinURL allows you to install Google AdSense-styled ads on your website. There are also a-ads, which allows you to earn money from ad impressions rather than clicks (so it's not PPC). This is a good way to make Bitcoins if you're a publisher, like a blogger or a webmaster.

3. Using Social Media

Some websites will compensate you for your work. Perhaps the most wellknown site in this category is CoinChat. For conversing on their site, it gives users a few milli-Bitcoins. These are completely random and are determined by an algorithm that considers your activity and how well you contribute to the current conversations.

A popular technique for Bitcoin enthusiasts to get money is to sell their forum signatures on Bitcointalk forums. There are a lot of advertisers that are prepared to do this, and selling signatures can be profitable for the socially engaged person who values contact on this topic (it's the same place where Satoshi Nakamoto first presented Bitcoin to the world).

4. Make your own Bitcoin Faucet and earn between $50 and $800 every month.

A bitcoin faucet is a project in which you construct a website or app for people to visit to receive bitcoins. You monetize the site with bitcoin-paying adverts. The adverts are paid in bitcoins for each page visit, click, or conversion.

You offer to split the revenue from the advertising with them, paying in Satoshi, which is bitcoin cents, to encourage many visitors to continue surfing the site daily and hourly. Users must earn a particular amount of Satoshi to claim their rewards, and payments are made weekly.

Faucets pay anything from 100,000 to 400,000 satoshi per hour. Some companies pay extra for seniority or task completion.

Faucets began to function only by completing captchas—a tedious activity for passive income. New faucets are popping up in games where users can earn satoshi by killing aliens, feeding creatures, or killing robots; the further they progress, the more they earn. As a result, this is a fantastic notion for your faucet.

The day will come when every video game player will be compensated for their time spent playing.

Take into account that bitcoin faucets frequently fail due to a lack of money or liquidity. The faucet's owners aren't getting paid quickly enough to keep up with the rising user base. They're also common targets for hackers.

Bitcoin Faucets Pay Out Small Sums

My first piece of advice was to make your faucet. If that's too difficult, consider joining one and receiving the rewards. Instead of making roughly $800 per month from a repetitive task, you'd be making $30 to $100 per month, but it's still money and a first step toward building up your bank account.

Keep in mind that bitcoin faucets are notorious for being unreliable and disappearing quickly. So join some respectable ones, such as Robotcoin.com and BitcoinAlien.com. These are also entertaining because they allow you to play games while earning money; my top recommendation is robot coin.

5. Make Money with Your Bitcoin Blog While You're Sleeping

Because bitcoin is so young compared to other targeted content types, there is plenty of room for new bloggers and websites. Every day, new bitcoin-related businesses emerge; everything from bitcoin exchanges, trading, play money sites, faucets, online shops, and mining compete for your advertising space.

Creating a bitcoin blog and monetizing it can take a long time at first, but consistent writing of high-quality content will attract advertisers in no more than nine months.

You can participate in affiliate schemes or open your bitcoin store. Bitcoin faucets, wallets, and exchanges all pay hefty referral commissions.

6. Make a Bitcoin-related product or service. Shop on the Internet

Bitcoin is still difficult to convert into US dollars or other tangible currencies. It's not impossible, but it does add extra fees and taxes to the procedure. Even so, it is still one of the most cost-effective ways to move money over the world.

Buying things with bitcoins is a terrific way to turn them useful while avoiding exchange fees and taxes. Especially if you can then resale the items and make some money.

Selling low-cost or bulk goods paid with bitcoin is a lucrative business option. All you need is a bitcoin merchant like BitPay.com for your Shopify or WooCommerce store. BitPay is already built into Shopify.

Bitcoins can be purchased in a variety of ways.

Bitcoins in your area

Exchanging bitcoins isn't the only way to invest in them. Local Bitcoins are frequently used to purchase BTC offline. The website's purpose is to bring together potential buyers and vendors. The seller holds the bitcoins in escrow and can only be released to buyers.

Purchasing bitcoins offline isn't always secure or trustworthy. As a result, it's best to meet the sellers during the day and bring a friend along in case things go wrong.

Bitcoin isn't merely a fad. Venture capital firms see Bitcoin as a viable alternative to traditional currencies in the long run. You can enter the world of bitcoin investment in a variety of ways. Coinbase, BitStamp, and Local Bitcoins are the most popular ways to invest in bitcoin in the United States, as previously stated. Do your research and figure out which path checks all of your boxes.

Bitcoin Purchasing Guide - A Simple 3-Step Process for Purchasing Your First Bitcoin

Many people have misconceptions regarding bitcoin, the world's first widely recognized and acknowledged cryptocurrency.

For example, many individuals believe that only hackers and nefarious characters utilize it. However, bitcoin is becoming more widespread, with companies such as TigerDirect, Expedia.com, Dell, and even Subway now accepting bitcoin payments.

What makes it so popular?

On the other hand, Bitcoin has several advantages over conventional currencies. You can, for example, send bitcoins to someone as payment without having to go through a bank (and get hit with extra fees). It's also a lot faster than using a bank wire or transfer to send money. You can send bitcoins to someone, and they will receive them in a matter of seconds.

With all of this in mind, it's no surprise that a large number of people are now attempting to purchase bitcoin for the first time.

120

It's not as simple as going to your bank and withdrawing bitcoins or as simple as going to a business and buying bitcoin with your hard-earned cash.

The system is a little more complicated than that. This Bitcoin Buying Guide will go over a few things you should know before purchasing Bitcoin so that you can do so safely and securely.

To begin with, while the price of a bitcoin may be above USD 2000 per coin, you do not have to purchase a complete bitcoin. You can usually buy a portion of a bitcoin for as little as $20 on most sites. As a result, you may start small and work your way up to gain experience with the system.

Second, this post is only for informational purposes and should not be construed as financial advice. Bitcoin is a dangerous investment, and you should contact your financial advisor before making any decisions.

So, here are three simple methods to purchasing Bitcoins:

1. get yourself a Bitcoin wallet.

The first step before purchasing bitcoin is to create a virtual wallet to store them. People can transfer their bitcoins using this wallet, a string of text.

Wallets come in various forms, including those you download to your phone or computer, online wallets, and even offline, cold storage wallets.

The majority of individuals would rather have a wallet on their phone or computer. Blockchain, Armory, Bitgo MyCelium, and Xapo are some of the most popular wallets.

It's usually as simple as installing the wallet as an app to your phone or downloading the software from the wallet's main website to your PC.

2. **Select a Purchase Location**

There are various types of stores to choose from, each personality. Certain internet vendors would sell you bitcoins for cash (or bank wire or credit card).

There are exchanges like a stock market where you may purchase and sell bitcoins from others. Local exchanges can also connect you with vendors in your region who want to sell.

There are also ATMs where you may make a cash transaction and have your coins delivered to your wallet in a matter of minutes.

Each bitcoin merchant has advantages and disadvantages. ATMs, for example, are fantastic for anonymity, but they charge up to 20% more than the current price, which is absurd. (On a $2000 BTC price, that's $400! So instead of $2000, you'll pay $2400.

Whatever you choose to buy from, make sure you do your homework and choose a reputable vendor with excellent customer service. First-time purchasers will have specific questions and require additional assistance with their first transaction.

Before you purchase, take your time and explore the many options. Coin prices, additional fees, payment methods, and customer service are all things to consider.

3. Purchase Bitcoin and deposit it in your wallet

Prepare your cash once you've discovered a place to buy (i.e. you may send a wire transfer or use your Visa to fund your account). Then you should wait for a good deal. (Bitcoin prices fluctuate 24 hours a day, seven days a week.) When you're ready, place your order.

You'll want to transmit your coins to your wallet once your order has been fulfilled and you've received them. Simply input your bitcoin address to request that the vendor send your bitcoins to you. They should appear in your wallet (depending on how fast the seller sends them out).

You are now the proud owner of a bitcoin. You can now transmit pennies to be used to pay for other goods and services or save them for a rainy day.

Last but not least, keep in mind that bitcoin is still in its infancy. There are significant price changes, and the currency is volatile. Never invest more money than you can afford to lose in bitcoins.

LENDING IN BITCOINS

Platforms for centralized crypto lending

Centralized, regulated exchanges are the "safest" option to lend your money. In this situation, the exchange operates as a middleman, ensuring that you get your money back plus interest.

Many exchanges offer a daily interest rate of roughly 0.003537 percent on BTC. While it may appear insignificant at first, this interest rate can add up to large earnings over time. The money flows to margin traders who borrow funds to fund leveraged trades on many of these exchanges.

Exchanges, as central authorities, can impose restrictions such as lock-up periods (during which you cannot withdraw your funds) and fixed interest rates. You must also supply extensive KYC information, which many people find unsettling.

Always double-check the exchange's security and legality, and you might earn 8-12 percent interest on your cryptocurrency.

DeFi Lending is a type of debt financing.

If the idea of centralized lending makes you cringe, DeFi platforms like Aave and Compound are the right alternative. DeFi lending uses smart contracts to execute loan conditions such as interest and repayment without middlemen.

Decentralised Finance (DeFi) financing becomes entirely trustless, permissionless, open-source, and (largely) safe as a result of this. Hackers can still use smart contract flaws to steal funds, as happened with the Poly Network incident in early 2021.

At the time of writing, DeFi protocols have a market capitalization of US$105.89 billion, making the sector robust and fluid.

DeFi lending is becoming popular since there are no restrictions on when to withdraw your funds, interest rates are often greater, and there are no KYC requirements.

Compound tokens are currently available for purchase on CoinSpot, and they grant you voting rights on technical and protocol changes, as well as other crucial decisions.

Peer-to-Peer Lending is a type of lending where people lend to each other.

P2P lending, unlike centralised and DeFi lending, which rely on established platforms to perform all of the heavy liftings, allows you to be more handson. You get to choose your interest rates, which means more profits and higher risks.

Peer-to-peer lending is made possible through services like BTCPop, which connect lenders and borrowers. It allows lenders to choose who they wish to lend their crypto assets to based on a reputation system (mostly in BTC).

It is the lender's job to assess each borrower. Even yet, they must accept full responsibility for defaulting debtors and the loss of their crypto assets.

Why Is Bitcoin's Price So Fluctuating?

A variety of factors causes variations in the Bitcoin spot price on Bitcoin trading exchanges. The Volatility Index, often known as the CBOE Volatility Index, measures volatility in traditional markets (VIX). Because cryptocurrency as a legitimate asset class is still in its early stages, there is no universally recognised index for Bitcoin volatility. However, we know that Bitcoin can experience volatility in the form of 10x price changes compared to the US dollar in a relatively short amount of time. The following are only a few of the many reasons that contribute to Bitcoin's volatility:

1. Negative press has an impact on ownership rates.

Geopolitical occurrences and remarks by government officials that Bitcoin is most likely to be controlled are among the news events that terrify Bitcoin consumers. Many bad actors were covered by Bitcoin's early adopters, resulting in headline news reports that stoked investors' greatest worries. The collapse of Mt. Gox in early 2014, and more recently that of the South Korean market exchange Yapian Youbit, have made headlines in Bitcoin news, as have other high-profile uses of Bitcoin in drug trades via Silk Road, which resulted in the FBI shutting down the market place in October 2013. All of these events and the resulting public panic caused the value of Bitcoins to plummet compared to fiat currencies. Nonetheless, Bitcoin currency investors saw all of these events as confirmation that the market was expanding, driving the value of Bitcoins vs the US dollar significantly up in the short period following the news.

2. Bitcoin's market value fluctuates.

Bitcoin shares several characteristics with gold. It is governed by a design resolution by the core technology developers to limit the quantity of BTC that can be created to a fixed amount, 21 million BTC. Because this differs significantly from fiat currency exchange, which is handled by government authorities who want to maintain low inflation, high employment, and acceptable growth through investment in capital assets, traders may designate more or less of their assets directly into Bitcoin as economies developed with fiat values show signs of power or weakness. The acknowledged store of value vs fiat money is one reason why Bitcoin may alter against fiat stock markets.

3. There is an excessive misunderstanding about Bitcoin's store of value and value mechanism.

Bitcoin's unpredictability is partly fueled by conflicting opinions of the cryptocurrency's implicit worth as a store of value and method of value transfer. A store of value is an asset that can be easily helpful in the future due to some predictability. A valuable store of value can be easily retained and exchanged for something better or more useful in the future. Anything or idea utilized to transfer property in the form of assets from one entity to another is referred to as a value transfer technique. Bitcoin's unpredictability makes it an uncertain store of value at the moment, but it assures nearfrictionless value transfer. Because these two drivers of Bitcoin's recent spot value differ from the US dollar and other fiat foreign currencies, we can see that Bitcoin's value can fluctuate in response to news events in the same way that fiat stock markets do.

4. The currency's massive owners have a small choice worth.

Bitcoin's unpredictability is influenced to some extent by holders holding large percentages of the currency's overall remarkable float. For Bitcoin traders with recent holdings of more than $10 million to see how they might convert such a large position into a fiat one without materially impacting the market. Because

Bitcoin's volume is comparable to that of a small-cap stock, it has yet to reach the mass market ownership levels that would be required to provide option value to large holders of the cryptocurrency.

NFT (NON FUNGIBLE TOKENS)

The non-fungible token (NFT) market has evolved into a significant part of the crypto business, with total spending on NFTs topping $12.6 billion, up from $162.4 million. While Ethereum is used to manufacture, buy, and sell most NFTs, hefty gas fees can make the process prohibitively expensive. According to data from Raribleanalytics, minting a single NFT on Ethereum costs roughly $98.69 in gas expenses, while minting NFT collections costs around $900.

To offset these expenses, many investors and developers try to sell their NFTs on secondary markets like OpenSea and profit. However, there are various ways to profit from NFTs other than selling them for more than you paid or developed them for.

CREATE AND SELL NFTS

Purchasing NFTs is "similar to investing in the stock market," according to Bossi: To put it another way, there are no assurances. NFTs are a risky investment when it comes to future gains. You can make an educated guess, but you never know what will happen, so it's crucial to do your homework before purchasing.

Make sure you do your homework on the artist or company making the NFT. They're more likely to be a legitimate business and perhaps a profitable investment if they appear to have a solid history of creating great work, a road map for continuing to create in the future, and a social media following of interested followers.

Non-fungible tokens and cryptocurrencies are emerging industries that entail considerable hazards and volatility. Before making any investments, think about your goals, risk tolerance, and time horizon.

The purpose of investing is to build wealth, and earning passive income is one of the finest methods to accomplish it. Simply said, passive income is when you invest in assets such as NFTs and have your money work for you.

Are you surprised to hear NFTs and passive income mentioned together? You're not the only one who feels this way. While the news is full of stories about NFTs selling like hotcakes, trading them isn't the only way to make money.

The truth is that blockchain-based assets like NFTs may provide a passive income in various ways, using ideas borrowed from traditional assets like bank deposits and real estate.

WHAT ARE NFTS, AND HOW DO THEY WORK?

Consider them tradable digital receipts maintained on a publicly distributed database known as a blockchain that everyone can access and independently verify at all times. These digital receipts contain unique information that can be used to verify who the only proprietors of certain tangible or immaterial goods are. However, it's important to note that NFTs don't save the digital entity they represent. Instead, they just direct you to the file's location elsewhere on the internet.

NFTs can be used to create passive revenue in a variety of ways. NFTs cannot be traded in the same manner as bitcoins since no two goods represented by them are ever the same. For this reason, they're referred to as "non-fungible" tokens.

A Non-Fungible Token, or NFT, is a one-of-a-kind means to own digital goods such as art, music, literature, or even Tweets. The irreplaceability of NFTs is what makes them valuable.

You can, for example, exchange one Bitcoin for another and obtain the same thing - a Bitcoin. You can't exchange one NFT for another and expect the results to be the same; they'll be different.

The Ethereum network is home to many popular NFTs, like the Bored Ape Yacht Club collection. As a result, ETH, an Ethereum-based coin, is utilized for payment and fees.

Furthermore, NFTs are assets, which means that their value can rise or fall depending on several factors, the most important of which is what another person is ready to pay for, similar to the worth of a work of art or a footballer.

As a result, the NFT trade is a popular strategy to profit. Some NFTs have been sold for as much as $69.3 million. NFT trade, on the other hand, is expensive due to Ethereum's astronomically high gas fees.

That's why, with concepts like renting, staking, yield farming, and more, many DeFi platforms offer many methods to earn passive revenue from NFTs.

NFTS ARE RENTED OUT.

Renting out your NFTs, especially ones in great demand, is one way to generate passive revenue.

Some card trading games, for example, allow players to borrow NFT cards to increase their chances of winning. Smart contracts manage the parameters of the arrangement between the two parties involved, as intended. As a result, NFT users typically choose their chosen rental agreement period and NFT leasing rate.

reNFT is an excellent example of a platform that allows users to rent or lend NFTs. This gives lenders the ability to establish maximum borrowing periods and daily rates, varying from 0.002 to 2 wrapped ethereum (WETH) on average.

The ERC-20 version of Ethereum's native ether is WETH (ETH).

Several GameFi platforms enable NFT owners to generate passive revenue by renting out their digital assets to other NFT players in the ecosystem. Smart contracts manage these rental agreements.

While NFT owners have complete control over the loan rate and length, many platforms cap on both, as you can see, this is a developing concept with a lot of potential in the future.

ROYALTIES FROM NFT

NFT Royalties NFTs are one of the most crucial cornerstones of the creatorled economy that Web 3.0 is aiming towards. NFT creators can earn royalties even after their art has been sold is an example. When the creator's NFT is exchanged on the secondary market, royalty fees provide passive income. The designer of the NFT sets these royalties.

What's the most enjoyable part? The process of earning passive revenue from NFTs is automated, as blockchain transactions are governed by smart contracts with royalty data pre-filled by NFT developers.

NFT creators can specify terms that impose royalty costs anytime their NFTs change hands on the secondary market, thanks to the underlying technology that powers them. In other words, even after selling their masterpieces to collectors, the makers can earn a passive income.

They will receive a part of the NFTs' sales price indefinitely if they do this. For example, if a digital artwork's royalty is set at 10%, the original creator will receive 10% of the total sale price each time the artwork is resold to a new owner.

It's worth noting that the authors frequently specify these predefined percentages while minting the NFTs. Smart contracts, which are selfexecuting computer programs that enforce commercial agreements, also regulate the entire royalties distribution process. As a result, as a creator, you won't have to worry about enforcing your royalty terms or keeping track of payments because the process is automated.

On NFTs, artists 'may set royalties.'

After the initial sale, creators who develop or "mint" their NFTs have a builtin chance to earn passive income. "You may establish royalties," adds Franck Bossi of NFT WatchDog, "typically 2.5 percent; some big projects, 10 percent to 12 percent."

This royalty is paid every time your work is resold on the secondary market.

NFTs are purchased and traded with cryptocurrency, most commonly ethereum. Latasha, a rapper who began selling NFTs of her videos in 2021, is now seeing her work on the secondary market. Her movie "MAKDA VERSE" was originally sold for 2.6862 ETH, which is currently worth $8,386 at the time of writing. It's now worth $3,468,453 on the secondary market for 1,111 ETH.

"Through NFTs, I'm witnessing myself become a millionaire," she recently told Grow.

It's 'the same as investing in the stock market' for collectors.

There are a few methods to generate money if you aren't a developer and are merely buying and selling NFTs:

Profitably sell an acquired NFT. If the price of an NFT rises after you purchase it, for example, you may be able to sell it for a profit. However, as with many collections such as comic books and records, it's difficult to predict which items will appreciate in the long run: All markets have the potential to move up as well as down.

Make passive money with a utility NFT.

Utility NFTs are rare and available in a variety of shapes and sizes. They can be, for example, a collection of related NFT paintings or an NFT game that builds on itself with further creations. When a utility NFT is sold on the secondary market, royalties may be paid to all of the utility's NFT holders. They'd receive royalties in a specific coin, which they'd then swap for cryptocurrency, most likely Ethereum.

Utility NFTs can be found by searching for them, particularly on platforms like OpenSea.

[Artists] can establish royalties, which are typically 2.5 percent, with some large projects ranging from 10% to 12 percent.

NFTS WITH A STAKE

Staking NFTs is one of five ways to get passive income from NFTs. To make passive revenue, staking involves locking or depositing your NFTs. The yield generated by staking is well recognized to be dispersed in tokens.

The ability to stake NFTs is one of the advantages of the marriage of NFTs and decentralized finance (DeFi) protocols. Some DeFi platforms require users to buy their native NFTs to stake them and then reward them with governance tokens that grant voting rights. Depositing, or "locking away," digital assets into a DeFi protocol smart contract to create a yield is referred to as staking.

While some platforms allow you to use any NFT, others require you to buy native NFTs to gain staking token incentives (which are usually priced in the platform's native utility token).

Platforms that make it easy to stake NFTs include:

- Kira Network is a social media platform that connects people
- NFTX
- Splinterlands
- Only1

In some situations, part of the benefits provided to stakeholders is denominated in governance tokens. These protocols provide token holders voting rights over how their ecosystems develop in the future. Most of the time, coins obtained through staking NFTs can be reinvested into other yieldgenerating protocols.

TO EARN NFTS, PROVIDE LIQUIDITY.

Several platforms have rewarded users that supply liquidity in exchange for NFTs. The owner of this NFT award can sell it to depart the liquidity pool soon.

A liquidity pool is a collection of digital assets locked in a smart contract and promised by many investors. The platform can leverage the locked pool of assets to disburse loans. It is now feasible to contribute liquidity and get NFTs in exchange to establish your position in a specific liquidity pool, thanks to the ongoing integration of NFTs and DeFi infrastructures.

For example, when you offer liquidity on Uniswap V3, the automated market maker (AMM) will issue an ERC-721 token, also known as LP-NFT, representing your part of the total amount locked in the pool. The token pair you placed, the tokens' symbols, and the pool's address are also carved into the NFT. You can sell this NFT to liquidate your liquidity pool stake swiftly.

ADOPT YIELD FARMING ENABLED BY NFT.

Yield farming using NFTs is a strategy in which investors seek to make additional returns by leveraging yields from one platform and investing them in another via methods such as staking. Users can now farm for yields utilizing NFT-powered products, as NFTs are quickly becoming a core component of AMMs. Return farming is the practice of combining several DeFi protocols to create the maximum possible yield from your digital assets.

AS SHOWN IN OUR EXAMPLE, the LP-NFT tokens provided as liquidity provider tokens on Uniswap can be used as collateral or staked on other protocols to generate additional yields. This potential opens the door to a multi-tiered income-generation approach appropriate for yield farmers. Consider it as a way to earn a yield on top of a yield-generating process.

However, consider that NFTs and the underlying smart contract technology are still in infancy. As a result, it's a good idea to complete your homework and grasp the hazards before implementing any of the aforementioned tactics.

You can establish royalties regarding passive income from NFTs. Artists who create NFTs can select a royalty rate and earn a passive income every sold.

Buyers can either sell an NFT once for a profit or purchase special "utility NFTs" that provide a passive income stream.

Non-fungible tokens can appear like they're all the rage. Since capturing the interest of the internet in recent years, investors and generally curious people have been trying to find out what they are and how they may profit from them. The fad has even caught the attention of celebrities.

NFTs are one-of-a-kind digital assets based on blockchain technology, such as films, pictures, or artwork. The latter is a public, digital database that keeps track of an asset's entire history. In the case of NFTs, the blockchain allows anyone to see exactly where they came from (say, a certain artist), ensures their uniqueness, and reveals their purchase and ownership history.

FREQUENTLY ASKED QUESTIONS ABOUT USING NFTS TO EARN PASSIVE INCOME

How does NFT help me make passive income?

Staking allows you to earn passive income from NFTs by locking or depositing them for a fixed length of time in return for yields paid in tokens or other digital assets.

Other options to create passive revenue from NFTs include royalties embedded in the smart contract while minting the NFT, renting NFTs to gaming platforms, and locking them in liquidity pools to collect incentives.

Is it possible to generate money with NFT?

Investors have been found to profit from NFTs through methods such as trading, in which one NFT is traded in exchange for cryptocurrencies. Other ways to get passive revenue from NFTs include:

- Depositing NFTs for a set period in exchange for rewards is staking.
- Allowing users or gamers on multiple platforms to rent an NFT for a set period and interest rate.
- Royalties: Receive royalty payments indefinitely whenever the
- NFT is exchanged (for NFT creators)
- Liquidity Pool: Participate in liquidity pools to earn incentives. Yield Farming: Reinvest incentives from one NFT passive income source into another for a higher return.

Non-fungible tokens (NFTs) are one-of-a-kind cryptographic assets that reflect ownership of a tangible or intangible object and act as value stores. The NFT becomes more valuable as the asset becomes more scarce. What's more, they're blockchain-based assets that may be staked just like other cryptocurrencies to generate significant profits.

IS A SPECIAL WALLET REQUIRED TO USE NFTS?

It all depends on the network you choose to create your token. Fortunately, most wallets now support Ethereum and Binance Smart Chain; thus, the difference shouldn't be significant. These are the two most popular blockchains for NFTs.

The most crucial thing to do here is to double-check the blockchain network on which your coin is constructed. If it's an Ethereum token, you'll need an Ethereum wallet that supports it. If it's on Tezos, you'll need a Tezoscompatible wallet.

You should always double-check that your wallet is compatible with the blockchain that your token is on.

I'm not sure which blockchain to utilize.

When minting an NFT, there are a lot of blockchains to choose from. The Ethereum blockchain was the first major blockchain to offer non-fungible tokens in the form we know them today. Binance Smart Chain, Polkadot, Tron, Tezos, and many other blockchains are now NFT-compatible.

Numerous NFT marketplaces and initiatives offer you access to a large pool of potential buyers. The majority of NFTs are now based on Ethereum or BSC. However, Ethereum's gas prices have rendered minting and processing NFTs prohibitively expensive. Binance Smart Chain is a considerably less expensive option with a better transaction speed.

WHAT IS THE BEST PLATFORM FOR MAKING NFTS?

Personal preference and the blockchain you want to utilize play a role in selecting a platform to mint your NFT. Most BSC protocols will generate your NFT as a BEP-721 token; therefore, it doesn't matter which one you choose.

It's usually ideal to use a platform with a marketplace you're familiar with if you want to exchange your token easily afterwards. You won't have to transfer your NFT to a separate location after minting it this method.

BakerySwap is the largest NFT marketplace, making it an excellent choice for anyone looking to sell their NFT after minting.

Treasureland offers free NFT minting. For minting your NFT, all of these BSC projects feature straightforward interfaces and low fees.

If you're considering using Ethereum, OpeaSea or Rarible are two of the most popular choices.

IS IT POSSIBLE TO MOVE AN NFT FROM ONE BSC MARKETPLACE TO ANOTHER?

Most BSC marketplaces and exchanges will accept both BEP-721 and BEP1155 tokens. These are the most common BSC NFTs you'll come across. If the new platform supports your token type, you may effortlessly move your NFTs between marketplaces.

While wrapping your tokens is an option, we advocate maintaining your NFTs on their native blockchain. What you can't do is transfer your NFTs to another blockchain marketplace. OpenSea, for example, does not support Binance Smart Chain NFTs natively.

Send the collectable to your wallet to transfer your NFT to another exchange. Simply transmit it to the relevant deposit address of the new platform once you've safely saved it. Always double-check that your NFT token standard is supported by your wallet and any platform where you intend to send it.

WHAT IS THE BEST WAY TO SEND MY NFT TO SOMEONE ELSE?

You can send your NFT to someone else directly from your wallet once you've purchased or created it. If your wallet includes an NFT section, you can simply select any of your NFTs and choose to transmit them (Trust Wallet and MetaMask offer this feature).

Please keep in mind that the recipient of your NFT must give you the correct deposit address for the sort of token you have. The recipient should send you their Ethereum ERC-721 deposit address from their wallet if you have an ERC-721 NFT on the Ethereum network.

IS IT POSSIBLE FOR ME TO SHARE MY NFT OWNERSHIP AND SELL REVENUES WITH OTHERS?

NFTs are now a bit hard when it comes to collaboration. There can only be one owner for the most prevalent types of NFT (ERC721, ERC1155, BEP721, BEP1155).

On the other hand, some initiatives want to share the revenues of an initial sale across numerous wallets. This feature is not included in the token's code and is dependent on the exchange or marketplace you use. Verify with the exchange you use to see if splitting the NFT's sale amount is possible.

You can use a decentralized platform like Featured by Binance to have complete control over your NFTs and store them in a non-custodial wallet.

Have fun minting! The non-fungible token ecosystem is rapidly expanding and becoming more accessible. Anyone interested in minting their own NFTs will find the process straightforward.

There's a project for you to utilize to make, purchase, or sell NFTs.

WHAT IS NFT STAKING, AND HOW DOES IT WORK?

Blockchains rely primarily on a global network of transaction validators to verify transactions before adding them to a blockchain block. Validators (or miners) are chosen depending on the cryptocurrency they promise to the blockchain network's operation. In exchange for contributing resources, miners receive incentives in the native cryptocurrency. The 'Proof-of-Stake' methodology of pledging crypto assets is known as'staking,' and the procedure is known as'staking.'

Similarly, you can donate NFTs to a project while earning passive income from awards or fees for committing the asset to a blockchain. Most NFT staking chances are currently available on play-to-earn gaming platforms like Decentraland, Sandbox, and Axie Infinity, among others. To stake, all you need is a bitcoin wallet that supports NFTs.

In-game NFTs, which players can purchase with cryptocurrencies, account for more than half of the NFT market. Since its inception in 2018, Axie Infinity, for example, has amassed a sales volume of over $2 billion.

However, it is crucial to note that not all NFTs can be staked. As a result, you should double-check the details before purchasing the NFT.

WHAT MAKES THE STAKING RETURN ON NFT SO HIGH?

When you stake an NFT, the staking platform calculates its value based on rarity and then calculates an annual percentage yield (APY). The higher the APY, the rarer your NFT is. An NFT's worth is also determined by its ability to create a consistent revenue stream, such as royalties.

WHERE CAN NFTS BE STAKED?

The following are the two most common staking platforms:

Onessus: All sorts of in-game NFTs from the Onessus blockchain games can be staked using the WhenStaking platform's currency, VOID. Depending on the staking time, it pays up to 80% APY on NFT staking.

Only1: This platform has a one-of-a-kind staking system focused on social interaction. It allows numerous users to stake $LIKE on NFT developers of their choice. The APY offered is higher if the creator has a high social media involvement with the investors.

There are a few others, including MOBOX and Zookeeper. Zionverse is a marketplace in India where you may buy digital assets and stake them to earn a profit.

NFTs are continue to wreak havoc on the crypto markets as businesses invest in their development. Before investing in NFTs or staking them, it's always a good idea to brush up on the foundations of cryptocurrencies and blockchains. Despite its infancy, NFT staking draws investors who high APYs may entice.

THE ADVANTAGES OF STAKING NFTS

1. **More money**: Investors in NFT staking lend their tokens to the blockchain network to exchange additional tokens that function as interest. The primary goal of staking is to earn incentives, which can be fungible platform tokens or newly created NFTs. For lending their NFT to another user and entering a liquidity pool, the collector or holder can earn up to 100% APY.

2. **NFTs in abundance:** Many staking sites for NFTs reward users with additional NFTs. Exclusive ownership benefits may be available with these new NFTs.

3. **Liquidity Has Increased:** The lack of liquidity is one of the drawbacks of non-fungible tokens. The liquidity of these uncommon assets improves due to NFT staking, which attracts additional investors.

NFTs are in high demand and have a high resale value. It's only natural for investors to earn passive income on their valuable assets while waiting for their value to rise. Staking your NFTmight not be your first thought for getting them, but it's a terrific way to boost your asset growth. Who knows, maybe you'll earn new NFTs with additional exclusive bonuses.

HOW TO MAKE NFTS AT HOME

If you haven't heard about the recent NFT (non-fungible token) craze, you must be living under a rock. Celebrities, digital artists, and other creatives are all preparing to publish their work on the blockchain. When it comes to minting NFTs, the choices are endless, ranging from artworks to melodies to collectable NBA trade cards. It's a terrific technique to prove creative work's validity and ownership.

Prices for your NFT can skyrocket if there's a lot of demand. You can also make some nice money if you're extremely talented (or lucky). Consider it a digital collector album or a one-of-a-kind painting. You may be familiar with visual artist Beeple, who just sold an NFT titled "Everyday: the First 5000 Days" for over $69 million.

In addition to Beeple, other artists are selling their NFTs on blockchain-based markets. The best-selling items speak for themselves.

Before you can start minting your own NFTs, you'll need three things:

- Whether it's a song, artwork, or a collectable,
- To pay the minting charge, you'll need some cryptocurrency.
- To store your bitcoin, you'll need a cryptocurrency wallet.

You'll also need to choose the blockchain on which your non-fungible token will be created.

TOKEN IN REAL ESTATE

Real estate tokenization is a modern extension of traditional fractional real estate ownership. It's a crowd-funding strategy that divides the value of a real estate investment into smaller portions to get over most of the investing roadblocks. A token is created for every fraction of the asset. For example, a $100 million piece of real estate can be divided into as many as 100 tokens, each worth a million dollars. Each of these tokens is encrypted with all relevant information that allows the investor to claim property ownership based on their share percentage. After then, the tokens can be purchased at their determined value and even displayed on a secondary exchange.

Real estate is one of the world's greatest asset classes regarding money invested. However, the startling $280 billion in real estate assets does not match the number of real estate investors. This is because the required capital is out of reach for small-scale investors. Second, real estate necessitates clumsy paperwork. The development of REITs in the early 1960s was an attempt to attract investors and modify the illiquid asset status of real estate (Real Estate Investment Trusts). A single property was divided into numerous sections, each held by a group of investors who pooled their funds, setting a precedent for tokenization in real estate. Transparency in asset management is becoming increasingly important.

WHAT IS TOKENIZATION OF REAL ESTATE?

Tokenization is converting real estate assets into several virtual (digital) tokens. The purchaser of a certain token becomes the owner of that share of the asset. These virtual tokens can then be sold on an internet marketplace.

Every token in real estate tokenization signifies direct ownership of an asset. These assets could be stock in a real estate company, a piece of real estate, or involvement in a real estate investment fund, among other things. As a result of tokenization, property buyers can conduct transactions digitally using tokens rather than relying on traditional paper documentation.

The goal of tokenization is to protect real assets, so it's also known as security tokens. Tokenization is the process of breaking an asset into tokens (shares) that represent a specific share of the underlying asset, similar to how securitization is the process of dividing an asset into shares.

Consider the following scenario:

Let's say you wish to tokenize a $50 million property with 500,000 square feet. If you divide the property into 500,000 shares, each share is worth $100 and represents one square foot of the property. When you tokenize a property, you divide it into square inches, and each token is worth $0.69.

The second approach, tokenization, obviously makes the property more available to a broader group of investors. To collect cash for a new wing or renovations, you can choose to limit the share offering to 20% of the total. The token will now be sold to investors in the following phase. As a result, real estate tokenization might be compared to corporate stock. The approach is similar to crowdsourcing, except that tokens are used and are available on the blockchain.

WHAT IS BLOCKCHAIN, EXACTLY?

Blockchain is a method of storing information (electronically in digital format) in such a way that it is difficult to manipulate or hack. A distributed database shared among the computer network nodes is known as the Hench blockchain. Bitcoins are the name given to it in the cryptocurrency world. Maintaining a secure and decentralized record of transactions is more efficient and easier using blockchain technology.

WHAT IS A BLOCKCHAIN, AND HOW DOES IT WORK?

Because real estate tokenization relies solely on blockchain technology, your tokens are extremely safe and secure.

TOKENIZATION OF REAL ESTATE: WHAT ARE THE DIFFERENT TYPES?

1. **Commercial Tokenization** is the practice of using legally compliant methods to tokenize the ownership of commercial properties.

2. **Residential tokenization:** For investors, asset owners, developers, and institutions, residential tokenization is the process of tokenizing fractional ownership of residential real estate.

3. **Trophy Tokenization** is the process of tokenizing real estate assets such as iconic buildings in prime locations with solid real estate foundations.

WHAT ISSUES DOES REAL ESTATE TOKENIZATION ADDRESS?

Why is it necessary to tokenize real estate? Tokenizing your real estate assets solves problems.

The pandemic has had an impact on economies all across the world. Inflation protection is a top priority for both institutional and retail investors. In the current economy, the only surefire method to stay afloat is to increase your investments in scarce assets, with real estate being the most rewarding of them all. Most ordinary investors cannot afford the capital required to invest in real estate.

Tokenization is a REIT innovation that aims to use blockchain technology to solve most of the challenges associated with this model. For the time being, tokenization appears to be the only viable alternative for most investors. The following are some of the obvious reasons for tokenizing real estate:

1. Real Estate Liquidity

Tokenization addresses real estate's most serious problem: asset liquidity. Liquidity is boosted via tokenization. In the old method, several parties are involved in the legal transfer of assets, but tokenization simplifies purchasing and selling real estate. It cuts out the middleman and enables direct ownership transfers from one investor to the next. Overcoming a liquidity shortage is one approach to increasing any asset's value. Tokenization can improve real estate liquidity by removing middlemen and the hefty transactions that would otherwise be involved.

2. Ownership Documentation

Legal ownership is demonstrated through legal documents that demonstrate the new investor's ownership rights. On the other hand, Tokenization is sharing and synchronizing a distributed ledger across various sites and making it available to multiple persons. In a couple of seconds, any modifications to the ledger are transferred to all participants. Each transaction is sent and authenticated to avoid issues originating from various ownership claims.

3. Searching for houses is a lot easier now.

Another issue that tokenization solves is the easy search for the property you want to invest in. Real estate assets could be tokenized and listed on a single centralized marketplace. Investors will search for potential investments in various geographic locations, and sellers will reach out to a larger number of potential purchasers. As a result, the investor's task is easier because searching for a suitable investment can now be done in one spot.

4. Transparency Increased

As previously said, tokenization is based on blockchain technology, so there are no concerns about security because blockchain is a well-proven technology. Transparency is boosted through tokenization. The distributed ledger on which tokens are held reduces the issue of indisputable proof of ownership but also helps to increase real estate market transparency. By digitizing your asset, you will gain complete protection and great transparency. With blockchain technology monitoring market mood, financial fronts, social environment, and operations, real estate's bankability improves significantly. The multidimensional technology used in the procedure makes future trend prediction more reliable. The investor's preceding due diligence, which would otherwise be time-consuming and costly, is practically removed.

5. Breaking Down the Barriers to Entry for Small Investors

Small investors would bring too much money for the conventional system to handle. As a result, marginal costs are occasionally higher than marginal revenue, resulting in a loss of money. However, because assets are divided into smaller amounts, and transactions take place in a virtual environment, tokenization lowers the barrier to entry for smaller investors. Furthermore, real estate tokenization allows investors to invest in real estate without the hassle of going through a lengthy legal process to transfer ownership.

6. Making Life Less Difficult

Tokenization Makes Things Easier. Blockchain technology transactions are faster and cheaper than traditional legacy financial systems because no middlemen are involved. Additionally, collecting rental payments automatically and distributing them to token holders has made life much easier. The strain on the investor is reduced through the digitalization of the process, increased automation, smart contracts, and the absence of third-party involvement. There is no documentation involved, and transactions take no more than three days. There are no downtimes because cryptocurrency exchanges operate 24 hours a day, seven days a week.

7. Reduced Transaction Costs

Because it uses blockchain technology to exchange tokens, tokenization reduces transaction costs dramatically. These tokens allow investors to sell and acquire real estate without paying the typical closing charges. Although a real estate investment trust (REIT) offers a similar value proposition, it has upfront fees and a high minimum investment requirement.

8. Tokenization Opens Up New Capital Channels

Tokenization expands investor access, particularly for small-scale investors. Smaller fractions of larger properties are cheaper, allowing retail investors to pursue new ownership opportunities. Furthermore, tokenization via blockchain removes geographical constraints for investors.

9. Counterparty Risk is Reduced via Tokenization

Tokenized real estate investments leverage smart contracts to eliminate the middleman, allowing only peer-to-peer transactions to take place. This considerably reduces counter-party risk and increases small-scale investors' confidence. The longer the chain, the more vulnerable it is.

THE MOST EXPENSIVE CRYPTO REAL ESTATE PROJECTS

Here are eight of the most promising tokenized real estate projects:

1. PROPY PRO IS A PRODUCT THAT PROPY DEVELOPED

Propy is an automated real estate platform whose major goal is to increase convenience while retaining the peace of mind of their customers as they process tokenized land that best meets their demands.

Smart contracts provide the foundation for the project's efficient and transparent operations. The project's target audience comprises both retail and institutional investors.

PRO is Propy's native token, created on the Ethereum network. The initiative thinks that real estate will inevitably become tokenized, and it offers the Crypto Real Estate Agent certification to help new investors get started. A knowledge assessment exam is administered after each certification. There are specific courses available on smart contracts and blockchain.

2. LABS

One of the most well-known names in real estate tokenization is the LABS organization. The G.A.I.N.S. concept is used to create these utility tokens:

G-Governance

A-Project accessibility

I-Incentives

N – "Nomination of Rights."

S- Staking a claim to a reward

The LABS group is dedicated to making real estate investment accessible to all types of investors. The LABS group's most recent project is the Kunang Kunang Glamping Resort in the heart of Indonesia. With LAB tokens, users can become owners of a tiny island in Indonesia for as little as 100 USDT.

The LABS groups' introduction of end-to-end crowd-funded initiatives makes the organization appealing to crypto users. Concerns concerning openness and communication between investors have been addressed via smart contracts. Thanks to blockchain technology, every part of real estate investment with the LABS Group is efficient and backed by expert research. For every real estate investment made with the LABS group, investors receive NFTs.

3. REAL ESTATE PROTOCOL IHT

The IHT Real Estate Protocol was created as a tokenized real estate investing platform to increase liquidity. The project aims to expand and diversify financial sources for safe real estate investments worldwide. HitBTC, Gate.io, and CoinW have listed three exchanges with their token.

IHT aims to create a "digital credit society" by combining blockchain and global real estate. Tokenization can disrupt an asset and lessen the owner and user gap.

The asset party that generates the real estate divide issues an Asset Tokenize Offer (ATO). The break is noted in IHT's kernel ledger. IHT requires the developer to disclose all essential information about the asset, including its location, ownership, and other factors. Investors can subscribe to ATO shares depending on appropriateness using the split products displayed on the IHT platform. Because of the secure and rapid transactions, instant liquidity can be expected.

IHT plans to tokenize $50 billion in assets, including tokenized lands from China, Europe, and Australia. Investors can expect 100 percent transparency and a shorter listing cycle with the digitization of real estate ownership.

4. ATLANT

ATLANT is one of the newest blockchain-powered tokenized real estate marketplaces. Uvas.com, a secure and regulated digital securities exchange forum, was created. This may better understand the project's risks and investment hurdles than most.

ATLANT has fulfilled the pre-requisites for the market's envisioned future with the launch of Redot, a digital asset exchange platform.

5. ETHERLAND

Etherland allows property owners to upload photos, papers, and vital information about their property and generate a unique NFT. These NFTS provide real-world property information. This enables the digitalization of property, subsequently tokenized and made available for purchase by platform users. Eliminating the intermediary increases the asset's liquidity and boosts investor trust in their decisions.

Its native token, ELAND, is traded on Uniswap, Pancakeswap, and Bilaxy, among other exchanges. A dedicated mobile application creates a property profile and a unique Land ID.

The various data linked with issued NFTs is one of Etherland's most appealing features. Users can easily select photos as the asset's information, making the trade secure and free of unnecessary regulation. The IPFS is linked to the NFTs released with ELAND currencies (InterPlanetary File System).

Investors can use Etherland tokens to access the Etherland Estatepedia, a unique real estate wiki. This database contains all necessary information on the assets with LAND IDs allocated to them. Many of the world's most iconic monuments, such as the Eiffel Tower and the Tower of Pisa, are listed for sale on the Etherland Estatepedia.

6. IMBREX

The initiative promises to be one of the forerunners of the real estate ecosystem's transformation. The goal of Imbrex, which is based on the Ethereum blockchain, was to offer owners complete control over sensitive information and the leads that resulted. Decentralization of the marketplace via blockchain-enabled the elimination of the intermediary. Transactions, data, and ownership are now more secure than ever, thanks to the InterPlanetary File System (IPFS).

Imbrex claims to be an excellent option for investors looking to save money because the platform does not charge for its services. The only additional expense is the transaction fee charged by Ethereum. Imbrex has over 2,200 project listings and is growing to cover worldwide properties.

7. UNITED

United's 'U' stands for utility. The project is planning to launch the world's first crypto metropolis in the future. UTED tokens can be used for various things, including grocery shopping and investing in tokenized real estate.

United recently announced the U-Cube platform, which intends to lower investment obstacles and expand crypto asset classes for UTED customers. Crowdfunding on U-Cube boosts liquidity and makes retail investing more accessible.

On www.u-land.com, the project recently featured over 300 ready-to-move-in apartments. UTED tokens can be used to own easily and invest in these properties. United platforms now only accept UTED and BTC token transactions. In the future, diversity will unlock the full power of the unchangeable system.

8. SYB COIN IS A CRYPTOCURRENCY THAT SYB CREATED

SYB Coin (SYBC) is a new digitized ecosystem project. The platform aspires to be a leader in transforming unused land into commercial and residential structures. SYBC tokens can then be used to invest in tokenized projects or buy out the entire company.

On the SYB forum, you can exchange Bitcoin, USDT, and Ethereum for local tokens. All portfolios of available projects are uploaded on the website, allowing potential investors to rent, lease, or buy assets. Middlemen are eliminated to improve transparency and efficiency, and smart contracts are implemented.

Because Nasdaq predicts a future boom in tokenized real estate, now is a good investment. Begin your study right now to discover more about the projects mentioned above, as well as many others. This will assist you in investing in the project that best meets your needs.

TOKENIZATION OF REAL ESTATE ASSETS: WHAT DOES THE FUTURE HOLD?

Do you know that worldwide commercial real estate investment reached an all-time high of $800 billion? Isn't it fascinating? The most liquid asset, real estate, necessitates more involved and lengthy transaction processes and considerable cash commitments. Everyone is concerned about keeping real estate transactions secure if they continue to be conducted digitally. Things are much easier to manage now that real estate holdings have been digitized. "Real Estate Tokenization" is the phrase we use to describe it.

The real estate industry has been embracing tokenization in recent years. "This is a word that many of you have never heard before. Most people are still ignorant that tokenization is a rapidly growing area of the financial industry that allows investors to invest in digital tokens backed by real-world assets and securities.

However, we've all grown accustomed to signing and submitting documents online; the next step is to ensure that every stage of the process is secure. As a result, "tokens" are used.

WHY IS TOKENIZATION THE REAL ESTATE INDUSTRY'S FUTURE?

Tokenization of real estate assets is the way of the future.

The market conditions are fast shifting due to the tokenization of real estate assets. Access is no longer restricted to only the most affluent investors. Investors can move their money more quickly, and asset owners can better manage their equity. Many more factors support real estate tokenization, demonstrating that it is the way of the future for real estate assets. Let's take a look at a few of the more important ones.

It improves the traditional real estate business by assuring greater market transparency, more accurate ownership tracking, increased liquidity, and the ability to invest in real-time.

Because tokens may be traded in real-time, it offers ambitious and innovative real estate businesses new opportunities.

Real estate tokenization is competitive with other well-known fundraising options such as venture capital and private equity.

In Europe, the United States, and Asia, tokenisation's technological and economic aspects have been properly addressed.

In the next five years, tokenization is expected to generate $4.2 billion in global real estate industry revenue.

These factors demonstrate that real estate tokenization is the way of the future. Compared to the old paradigm of dealing with properties and investors, this process offers greater flexibility, increased security, and incredible versatility.

WHAT IS THE BEST WAY TO TOKENIZE YOUR PROPERTY?

To begin, it is critical to comprehend what a token represents. The token is nothing more than a digital share. Its economic rights are the same as those of any other share. A token can represent collateralized debt ownership, an equity position in a legal business, a portion of a deed, or any other type of real estate asset.

The sponsor can generate finance for a real estate project by offering to issue shares in token form or offering investors the option of exchanging shares for tokens in an upstream business. The initial real estate tokenization process is similar to crowdfunded real estate deals, except that the transaction is digitized.

With tokenization, sponsors either complete the necessary regulatory processes to allow private or public trading of the tokens or offer investors the option of exchanging their shares for tokens from another organization that has completed those steps. Once the investor's stake has been tokenized, it is digitally recorded on a blockchain and sold on secondary markets via the ATS. Investors have the option of selling all or part of their interest. They can also choose to keep their tokens for the duration of the investment lock term. Investors in this situation receive their portion of distributions throughout the investment lifecycle, just like non-digital shares.

We've broken down the process of tokenizing a real estate asset into five stages to make it easier to understand. Let's have a look at those steps.

Processes Involved in Tokenization of Real Estate

TOKENIZATION OF REAL ESTATE IN 5 STEPS

1. Deal Organizing

It is the first phase, during which different criteria such as asset kind, shareholder type, jurisdiction, and applicable legislation play a vital influence. The asset's owner selects the precise property or properties to be digitized. In most cases, issuers choose to tokenize an existing deal to provide liquidity to current investors before raising funds for a new project.

2. Digitization (Legal Structure)

Information previously saved on paper or in document form is uploaded to the blockchain during the digitization step. Smart contracts store this data, and security tokens are created. To put it another way, the digitization of real estate necessitates the creation of a legal wrapper around each particular property to securitize and create an investment vehicle.

To date, the most prevalent structures we've seen are

Tokens represent a single asset Special Purpose Vehicle (SPV) shares under this structure. This structure is only available to accredited investors or approved institutional buyers.

The token here symbolizes units in a real estate fund, a private equity company that invests in a portfolio of properties. The tokenized fund interest can only be leveraged by accredited investors or approved institutional buyers.

Tokenization is an extremely effective technique of generating funding for projects. Tokens are made available to both retail and accredited investors in this situation.

Real Estate Investment Trust (REIT) - While REITs are expensive to run, they have one major advantage: they are open to retail investors. Investors in REITs can issue digitized shares, and token holders have the same rights to the REIT's operational revenue that traditional investors do today.

3. Selecting Technology

After you've decided on a deal structure or legal structure, you'll need to make some technical considerations. The following are the four primary choices you must make:

Selecting a Blockchain / Token - choose the blockchain on which the token will be recorded, as well as the data and transfer limitations that will be included in the token.

Custody - A secure custody solution is required to store real estate tokens properly.

Investors' KYC/AML verification is necessary, and prospective investors might be issued digital securities.

Primary/Secondary Markets — Where do you want digital securities presented to potential investors through primary issues or major secondary exchanges? This judgment indicates if the capital raise will be successful and whether investors will access liquidity.

Using AlphaPoint's Exchange technology, many large operators began to build their marketplace.

4. Marketing and Distribution

The creation and distribution of tokens is the focus of this phase. Different payment methods, such as cryptocurrencies, stablecoins, fiat currencies, and others, are accepted for purchasing digital tokens. A live sale can be held to sell these tokens to investors. The investors will need a digital wallet to store the tokens available on both the web and mobile.

Tokenized Asset Distribution and Marketing

Primary Distribution is the process of distributing exchange for investment capital tokens to investors and recording their information on a digital ROM.

Corporate action management processes, such as shareholder voting and dividend distribution, are part of post-tokenization management. Smart contracts coded on the token can automate these processes. The posttokenization management will continue until the tokens mature or are redeemed.

Secondary Trading- The advantage of tokenization in improving liquidity is recognized through secondary trading. Here, a token holder can trade tokens with another investor over the counter or exchange.

5. After the Support

Additional support is provided to investors in mortgage issues, regular tracking of all token holders' activities, forming a corporate code, and dealing with legal difficulties. We hope you've grasped all of the steps involved in tokenizing the real estate asset.

TOP REAL ESTATE TOKENIZATION BENEFITS

Tokenization of Real Estate Has Many Advantages

Fractionalization

Tokenization lowers the entrance barrier for assets that need a big amount of upfront funding. The asset's interests can be more easily shared among a larger group of investors, democratizing access to the asset. A digital register of members (ROM) on the blockchain securely manages fractional ownership.

Efficiency in Operations

'Smart contracts,' or programmable activities on the blockchain, make it easier to automate tasks like investor whitelisting, compliance checks, and post-issuance issues like dividend distribution.

Flexibility

One of the most significant benefits of real estate tokenization is that everyone can invest a specific amount and become a partial property owner, profiting from the gains. The token holder can easily sell these tokens for a higher price on the secondary market. Tokenization is, without a doubt, a better solution for crowdfunding because it gives the user instant digital ownership.

Fraud is being reduced.

No one can change the transaction because it is recorded digitally on blockchain technology. As a result, tokenization gives real estate investors more trust and confidence.

Settlement Time is Cut in Half

Transactions in tokenized products can be settled faster than typical finance transactions. Unlike traditional transactions, which can take days or even weeks to clear, tokenized transactions can be finalized quickly.

The world is watching cryptocurrencies and NFT, startled by their great security and flexibility in digital asset management benefits. At this time, blockchain has provided real estate owners with fantastic opportunities by facilitating 'Real Estate Tokenization.

The digitization of real estate assets relies on blockchain technology. A blockchain development company can provide hassle-free tokenization solutions for your properties by providing a trustworthy tokenisation platform.

CONCLUSION

When you invest your hard-earned money in the market, your main goal is to build up your wealth and become financially secure.

One way to make sure your investments aren't all the same is to have different types of investments in your portfolio, like real estate, equities, bonds, mutual funds, and exchange traded funds.

Whatever financial instruments you choose, the idea is to get to a place in your life where you can rely on your investments to generate fresh income. Or, to put it another way, to make money while you sleep. To do so, you must construct a portfolio in which your money works for you.

However, generating a strong and consistent high-yield passive income is difficult, particularly in volatile markets.With the enormous fluctuations that occur in every asset class, you must build a new passive income stream on which you can count. Before you can build up numerous passive income streams, you must first understand what passive income is.

Passive income is defined as income that requires little or no effort to earn and maintain. This could range from renting out a room or a whole property to collecting profits from stocks.

Interest earned on bank deposits is another type of passive income (though inflation is rapidly devaluing it).Recently, crypto (along with nft) has spawned a completely new method of creating high-yield passive income. Essentially, passive income is any income that rises without much of your effort.

Creating several income streams allows one to have multiple cash flow sources, eventually breaking away from their day job. With a lot of passive income sources, you will be better able to deal with a loss when one source doesn't work,

There is only so much money a person can produce in a single day, which is why it is necessary to invest the additional money you do have in methods that will generate more money.

You don't want to work harder; you want to work smarter-to create a growing and sustainable income that grows around the clock, whether you're at work or lounging on the beach.

Remember that the average American millionaire has six different sources of income.

Milton Keynes UK
Ingram Content Group UK Ltd.
UKHW052045200324
439609UK00005B/122